MARKETING STRATEGIES FOR SMALL BUSINESSES

by Richard F. Gerson, Ph.D.

THE **CRISP**
SMALL BUSINESS &
ENTREPRENEURSHIP
SERIES

CREDITS

Editor: Beverly Manber

Layout/Design: ExecuStaff

Cover Design: Kathleen Gadway

Library of Congress 92-54355
ISBN-1-56052-172-4

INTRODUCTION TO THE SERIES

This series of books is intended to inform and assist those of you who are in the beginning stages of starting a new small business venture or who are considering such an undertaking.

It is because you are confident of your abilities that you are taking this step. These books will provide additional information and support along the way.

Not every new business will succeed. The more information you have about budgeting, cash flow management, accounts receivable, and marketing and employee management, the better prepared you will be for the inevitable pitfalls.

A unique feature of the Crisp Small Business & Entrepreneurship Series is the personal involvement exercises, which give you many opportunities to apply immediately the concepts presented to your own business.

In each book in the series, these exercises take the form of "Your Turn," a checklist to confirm your understanding of the concept just presented and "Ask Yourself," a series of chapter-ending questions designed to evaluate your overall understanding or commitment.

In addition, numerous case studies are included, and each book is cross-referenced to others in the series and to other publications.

BOOKS IN THE SERIES

DEDICATION

This book is dedicated with much love to my family and to all my clients who have benefitted from these marketing techniques and to those businesses that will now benefit.

CONTENTS

CONTENTS (continued)

CONTENTS (continued)

CONTENTS (continued)

PREFACE

Small businesses seem to have a tough time making it regardless of the state of the economy. Business owners are concerned with so many things—employees, suppliers, operations, laws, regulations, taxes, their families and who-knows-what else. They rarely, if ever, have time to do the one thing that would make their business successful. Whatever else a business owner does, he or she must market!

Marketing is not some ephemeral or ethereal thing that cannot be touched, felt or quantified. On the contrary, marketing can be designed and measured. You can use it to learn exactly who your customers are, where they are coming from, how much they are spending with you and what else you must do to reach them. Marketing can also help you get new customers, keep current ones and even "steal" customers from your competitors. Marketing is the engine that drives your business.

Since most small businesses cannot compete with the mega-corporations and their marketing budgets, there must be a way to level the playing field. This book identifies that way. *Marketing Strategies for Small Businesses* identifies hundreds of ideas, methods and techniques that you can use to market your small business effectively and successfully. And, best of all, every one of these techniques is either a low-cost or a no-cost technique.

This book will tell you how to mail your direct marketing pieces for free, buy national advertising space for 25 cents on the dollar, get the best consultants in the world to work for you for free, double and triple your sales force without spending a dime, get thousands of dollars worth of advertising for free, get other people to promote you and your business, get and keep customers for life, determine exactly how much a customer is worth to your business so you can determine exactly how much you can spend to get a new customer and develop word-of-mouth marketing program. You will learn how to do all this and more.

The book provides hundreds of what I call Maverick Marketing™ strategies, tactics and techniques. All have been tested and validated. They work, and they work especially well for small businesses. You can implement them as they are presented or make modifications to suit your business.

The book begins with 10 great ways to market your business and get it off to a flying start. There is no theory here, only practical advice. Other chapters discuss how to build your image and reputation, do direct marketing, use direct mail and word-of-mouth, advertise and buy media space, improve your selling skills and provide superior customer service. The book includes a brief, but invaluable, chapter on back-end marketing, where you continue to go back to your customers to sell them additional products and services.And, you will learn how to write a marketing plan to guide your business.

Good luck. Your small business can be successful, regardless of the economy, your competitors, your advertising budget or what people tell you. All you have to do is implement some of the marketing strategies and tactics described in this book, and watch your business take off. Call or write to me and let me know how you are doing or if you have any questions.

Richard F. Gerson, Ph.D., CMC

CHAPTER
ONE

START

MARKETING

THE 10 GREATEST MARKET- ING TECH- NIQUES

Most marketing books start you off with basic information and definitions about marketing and tell you what to expect from the rest of the book. While this practice has proven to be tried and true, and has helped sell a great many books, that is not what we are doing here.

You are a business owner. You need advice and information that will help you make money right now, without having to wade through pages of introductory material. With that and you in mind, here are what I consider to be the 10 greatest small business marketing techniques of all times.

Use these strategies or techniques to start making money from your marketing efforts. But, before you run headlong into a full-scale marketing campaign, read the rest of the book. See how the other strategies and techniques complement these 10. Use the techniques and you will be the most successful marketer and small business owner in your area, if not in your industry.

Many small businesses are scrambling, trying to get new customers and trying to outdo their competition. Some spend lavish amounts of money on advertising and promotions to attract new customers or offer deep discounts to keep their cash flowing. Neither of these approaches is profitable nor wise, especially for a small business. You will never have to do this if you develop and implement a marketing plan that includes one or more of the following 10 small business marketing techniques.

These techniques will work, regardless of the economic conditions in your industry. Do not be fooled by their simplicity. They are powerful and effective marketing strategies and techniques. Be glad that you will know about them while your competition is still in the dark. If you use these strategies and market your small business properly, you will rarely feel the effects of a recession, and you will profit greatly during positive economic conditions.

Ten Marketing Techniques to Make Your Small Business More Profitable

1. Unique Selling Proposition (USP) and Unique Marketing Position (UMP)

Your USP is why people purchase your products or services. It makes your small business unique and differentiates you from your competition. Your UMP is the position you hold in their minds, such as being the friendliest small business in town or the most service-oriented or the lowest price provider. Most businesses do not have either of these important factors. Having both a USP and a UMP will place you significantly ahead of your competition, which will be forced to play catch-up.

Since most businesses never think about a USP or UMP, you may not have either or both of these important statements. Look at your competition. See what they are doing. Find out why people buy from them—learn what their USP and UMP are, if they have them. Ask their customers why they buy from your competitors. Then, ask *your* customers why they buy from you.

Use this information to formulate your USP and UMP statements. The key is to identify the primary factor that differentiates you from everyone else—what you do better than anyone else. Figure out what you do for your customers, what need you satisfy, and make that your USP. Figure out how your customers perceive you. If you are satisfied with that perception, make that your UMP.

Your Turn

Write your USP and UMP statements:

► USP:

► UMP:

---

2. Recall and Reactivation Programs

Recall and reactivation programs are designed to get back former customers or get inactive customers buying from you again. These programs involve contacting customers whom you have not seen for some time—three to six months or a year. Call or write them to find out how they are doing. Invite them in for a special program or sale. If they come in within a specified time to buy from you, offer them a small gift as an added value to their purchase.

Remember that former customers are your gold mine. You just need to remind them about your products or services, what you do for them and how well you do it. Recalling and reactivating former or inactive customers is always easier than finding and acquiring new customers. The cost of recall and reactivation programs is minimal, compared to overall new customer acquisition costs. Once you have them back, it is essential that you convert them to loyal, repeat customers.

Your Turn

Answer the following:

► What are you doing now, or what will you be doing in the immediate future, to implement recall and reactivation programs?

---

3. Customer Recognition and Reward Programs

To be successful, your small business needs referrals and positive word-of-mouth advertising. You can help this along by showing your appreciation for customers who buy from you and who refer new customers to you. You can do this through a referral reward program and a frequent shopper reward program for your customers. Put their names up on a "Thank You" bulletin board in the store or office. Send cards and letters thanking them. Call them personally to thank them and invite them in for a special offer. (For more information see Chapter 11.)

As your customers continue to refer or buy, send them gifts of progressively increasing value. This tiered reward program shows your customers and referral sources you care about them and appreciate their efforts. An alternative would be to give them increasingly greater discounts on purchases, based on the number of people they refer or the number of purchases they make.

Customers appreciate business owners who appreciate them. Send your customers holiday and birthday cards, congratulatory letters, and thank you cards or letters when they refer new customers to you. Show them you care about them personally, and they will return the favor by referring customers to you, purchasing more from you and remaining loyal to you.

A note of caution—as part of their show of appreciation, some small business owners send their customers wedding anniversary cards. I recommend that you stay away from these cards. Your loyal customer may be separated or divorced, and your attempt at showing appreciation may backfire.

Your Turn   **List the recognition and reward programs you are now using for your customers, or those you would like to use.**

▶ Recognition

▶ Reward

4. Letter of News

Newsletters enable you to keep in touch with your customers while you keep them informed. People often receive many newsletters, and yours might simply add to their pile of "junk" mail. This suggestion will help your information stand out from the crowd. It also keeps your name in front of the customers.

Send them a letter of news. A letter of news is a personal letter to customers that contains all the information you would normally put in a newsletter, but is personalized. How do you personalize it? Just merge the information from the letter of news with the names and addresses on your list or database of customers. Include a personalized salutation, such as "Dear Richard," from the database merge, and write the letter of news as if it were a newsletter.

Do not worry about the length of the material. People will read personal letters of any length much faster and more completely than they will anything else, including a newsletter. They will reread it if they are interested in the material.

5. Charity Tie-Ins and Community Service

Get involved with a local charity or sponsor a community event or sports team. Volunteer your services for a committee or an advisory board. Make donations to charities and make the event public. Your charitable contributions, civic support and civic-mindedness will be rewarded. Customers like to do business with companies that give back to the community.

Your Turn

List all the charities, civic organizations and youth sports league sponsorships you are involved with. If your list is blank, look for something to support right away.

► Do these first five marketing strategies make sense to you? Do you use any of them now? If so, which ones? How effective have they been for you?

► What can you do to improve on your current marketing efforts, especially if you were to stop reading right here?

► What are some of your most effective and greatest marketing strategies?

6. Public Image, Identity and Reputation

The image and identity you create for yourself and your business will follow you. Be visible in your community. Join business groups, service organizations and other clubs. Write articles, give speeches and send out press releases on newsworthy events related to your business. Be available to customers, and always speak to the media if they call. Remember that your public image is only the perception people have of you at a given moment. Your public identity is the physical, mental and emotional embodiment of that image all the time. It is who and what you and your business are in the minds of customers.

Your reputation is what your customers tell their friends and associates, which is quite different from your image and identity. An excellent reputation usually results in positive word-of-mouth advertising and increased referrals. A negative reputation can hurt you tremendously.

Your Turn

Answer the following:

▶ You have the choice between having a specific image in the minds of your customers or having an excellent reputation—which do you choose?

- My company's public image is:

- My company's public identity is:

- My company's reputation is:

---

7. Direct Response Advertising

Too many entrepreneurs and small businesses advertise in print, on radio and television, using "institutional" or "tombstone" ads. These are technical or informational advertisements that do nothing to motivate the customer to call or come into your place of business and buy. Often, these advertisements are run to massage somebody's ego, rather than to get business.

Institutional advertisements are image advertisements. As a small business, you cannot afford to run these. Your advertisements, including your *Yellow Pages* advertisement, must be sales pieces that motivate customers to call, write or come in to buy something. Once they contact you, ask for their name, address and telephone number—at a minimum—to track the effectiveness of each advertisement. Track to make certain you get a good return for your advertising dollar. How else will you know if your advertising is creating the response you desire? All advertising must be direct response.

8. Sampling, Discounts and Coupons

Businesses give away free samples of products or services all the time. They also offer discounts and coupons to motivate people to try their products or services. This is especially true when they are offering something new to customers and want to see how customers will respond. When the business wants to move an item that has not sold well, a "special sale" (read discount) is offered on the item as a "loss leader" to get people into the store or business. The business manager hopes that the customer will be sold additional items or a more expensive replacement product.

As long as it is cost effective, always consider doing this. The return on this investment—that is, customers making subsequent purchases—must be sufficient to support a sampling, discount or coupon program. Some small businesses consider the program successful if they are able to capture the information they need about the customer and use it later for future sales purposes.

9. Service Guarantees

Whatever type of small business you are in, or whatever type of product, program or service you provide, give your customers a guarantee. Base your guarantee on the product or service, its cost to you to produce and sell and the quality of it—the higher the quality, the lower the possibility of a customer using the guarantee.

Make the guarantee full money back and unconditional, no strings attached. Do not make your customers jump through hoops to return something. If they are dissatisfied with what you sold them, they are just unhappy or they merely want to exchange it for another item, let them. The implementation of the guarantee should be easy for everyone.

When customers see that you support your sale, the majority of them will honor their purchase. People will appreciate the confidence you have in your product or service, and they will feel comfortable with you because you take all the risk. Only a few people will take advantage of your service guarantees. Cater to these people and give them what they want. They will continue to do business with you as long as you provide them value for their money.

Make your customer service systems easy to use. For the guarantee to work, the systems must be more than complaint handling. They must be designed to ensure customer satisfaction at all times. Employees must be trained and empowered to take responsibility and make decisions that will ultimately help and satisfy the customer. Once customers are satisfied and see you will support your guarantees, they will do more business with you.

The reason for this is simple—you have reversed the risk. Customers have nothing to fear when they buy from you. If they do not like what they buy, they can return it and get their money back or make an exchange. You bear the cost of selling it to them in the first place, and you bear the cost of accepting the return.

If you do business by mail, or through a shipping service, never make the customer pay for return postage or shipping—you bear that cost also. This way, you completely take the risk from the customer, and customers love to do business with people who truly believe in and stand by their products or services.

10. *Everybody Sells and Everybody Services*

This is a mental attitude you must impart to your entire staff. Everybody markets, everybody sells and everybody is responsible for servicing and satisfying the customer. Sales and service are inseparable in business today, because customers are demanding more value and support for their purchases. Your entire staff, or you alone if you are an individual entrepreneur, must always be selling and servicing.

Successful sales professionals know how to identify their customers' needs, expectations, wants and satisfiers. These sales professionals also market their products or services so that the job of selling becomes easier. They listen to customers more than they speak to them, work with customers to achieve a win-win solution for everyone, and service their customers to the best of their abilities. They hope to exceed their customers' expectations.

In short, successful small businesses market and sell their products and services in ways that develop rapport, trust and long-term relationships with their customers. Achieving these outcomes is the way to retain customers for life.

Summary

These are the 10 greatest small business marketing techniques. Obviously, there are many more marketing strategies that will work for you, as you will learn while reading this book. However, research and experience has shown that these 10 are the most cost effective—you can spend a little and make a lot.

Small businesses across the country, from individual entrepreneurs and consultants to companies with millions of dollars in revenue, have been taught to use these strategies and tactics as part of their marketing programs. Their success has been unparalleled. Use one, a combination or, preferably, all 10—you will realize tremendous success in your small business.

ASK YOURSELF

 ▶ Describe the small business marketing techniques that you use.

IMAGE-BUILDING MARKETING STRATEGIES

CHAPTER TWO

PROMOT- ING YOUR BUSINESS

Let us assume you either have all your licenses, identification numbers, permits and anything else you need to operate your small business or you will get them shortly. You must now tell the public—your prospects and potential customers—who you are, where you are, what you do and how and why you do it better than anyone else. You do this through marketing.

Again, we are not talking about traditional marketing or marketing theory. We are talking about unique and different approaches that work. Everything that follows has been applied successfully in more than 100 industries. You just need to modify it to fit your business and make it work for you. These techniques are the only ones you should use to build your company image. Never use image advertising—the costs are prohibitive.

TYPICAL MARKETING TECHNIQUES

There are some basic marketing techniques that will work to get your name out in front of the public and let customers know they should do business with you. Follow these inexpensive and effective image marketing techniques as they are presented. They will bring customers to you. If you adapt them, make sure your modification improves them and you are not changing them just to gratify your own ego. These same techniques are used by the largest companies all over the world. Certainly they can be used by your small business.

Press Releases Build Both Images and Reputations

Everyone is familiar with a press release, the most common marketing/public relations technique. It is a simple way of conveying information about your business to the media, whether it is to newspapers or radio or television stations.

Simply write up a press release and send it to your local media. The release should contain information on your business, what you do, when you are doing it, how you are doing it and the products and services you offer. Your press release should tell the media something newsworthy about yourself, your business or something you have done.

You can achieve almost instant success in getting a news release placed in the newspaper by sending an office/store/business opening release or a new client release. If you have never sent one, regardless of how long you are in business, this initial release is only an announcement, not a sales presentation. Tell the media about your business, who you are, where you are located and how you will serve customers, or who your new client is.

With the release, you may want to include a picture of yourself and/or your facility or location. Make sure the picture has something to do with the release. For example, people who get promoted and send a press release to the newspaper have a better chance of getting that release printed if it is accompanied by a picture. Press releases with pictures tend to get printed more often and are responded to more rapidly by radio and television media.

The format and contents of the basic press release shown on the next page has never failed yet; there is always some mention of the business in the publications that receive it.

Change the words and content to suit your specific needs or situation, but follow the format. Remember that in this release and in any other release you write, the material should be newsworthy. Newspaper editors and assignment editors at radio and television stations do not have time to read any press release that does not have something newsworthy to say. You can really make friends if you send them only items of value, rather than just sending releases to see how many times you can get your name in the paper or mentioned on the news.

In your releases, go from the specific to the general. The media may not have time to read your entire release; get them the most important information in the first paragraph or two. Include the who, what, when, where, how and why of your press release in these two paragraphs. Keep all releases to one or two pages. This information will help get you started. Chapter 4 discusses press releases again and includes ten of the most important topics that interest the media.

NEWS RELEASE

DATE: Today's Date
CONTACT: Richard F. Gerson
TELEPHONE: (xxx) xxx-xxxx

FOR IMMEDIATE RELEASE

NEW CLIENTS OBTAINED

Safety Harbor, Florida—Gerson Goodson, Inc., a marketing and management consulting firm, has been retained by ABC, Inc. to provide marketing, public relations and training services. ABC, Inc. sells . . . products and services and can be reached at xxx-xxxx. For more information call Richard Gerson at (xxx) xxx-xxxx.

###

Notice several things about the preceeding press release.

► The important information is right at the beginning.

► You might go a step further and describe one important benefit or unique aspect of your small business, which would make the release even more interesting to the media and the reading public.

► The telephone number to call is included twice in the press release. You want to make sure that those who receive your press release, as well as those who will read it in a newspaper, know how to contact you.

► The standard press release points to a second page with the direction "-MORE-" (see pages 43-44); end the release with the symbol "###". This is the basic convention used in the industry.

Follow the same formula for all your press releases. Put yourself on a schedule to send out a release every month, every quarter or every six months. The key is to keep your name and business in front of the media and the public. Just remember that the press release must have something newsworthy in it or the recipients will file them in the garbage as soon as they receive them.

Press releases are one of the least expensive marketing techniques you can use. They are also one of the most effective. For the price of paper and a postage stamp, you have the possibility of receiving what amounts to free advertising in newspapers, on radio or on television, just by the fact that your name or business gets mentioned. You cannot buy that kind of publicity.

Depending on your type of business, you may not want to limit your marketing to your local area. To create a national image and reputation, send your releases to trade magazines, professional associations and trade newsletters. Put other people in your industry on your mailing list—even your competitors, depending on how much you want them to know. You never know who will receive a press release and pass it along to someone else who may want to do business with you.

If you have ever written and mailed out a press release, get a copy of it. If you have never written a press release, write one now. Compare its format and style to the criteria described above. Once you have done that, read the sample press releases on pages 17 and 43.

▶ How similar is your press release to the samples?

- Do you go from the specific—most important points—to the general—least important points?

- Is your press release set up so the editor can delete from the bottom up?

- Can the reader of your press release get the basic idea from reading just the first sentence or two?

*If you answered **no** to any of these questions, rewrite your press release. It takes practice to get good at this type of writing. This is also why businesses and companies pay marketing and public relations experts well to get them favorable media coverage.*

IF YOU DO SEMINARS OR SPEECHES

Many newspapers publish a section called a calendar of events. The calendar is a listing of upcoming events and activities in the local area, such as seminars, talks, meetings, health fairs, open houses, etc. The listing is free if you send the information in writing to the paper. The only requirement is that you usually have to mail it about two weeks before the event. Often the information must be sent to a specific person. Get to know this person so that when you are hosting something at your facility or office, or doing something such as a seminar for the general public, they will look at and publish your event release first. Calendars of events publish information on a space-available basis, and it is often first in, first printed.

DON'T FORGET THE LITTLE GUYS

You have canvassed the telephone books, made your telephone calls, identified your contacts, made your personal introductions, started your database, and developed your primary media list. Now you are ready to send out some releases. Wait! Your list is not complete.

Some of your best publicity will come from little newspapers. These are the ones that are thrown on your driveway for free, weekly or monthly. Quite often, these small local papers are more than happy to get information about your small business and are thrilled to print it.

Get to know the editors and publishers of these papers. Send them releases at the same time you send to the major players. Smaller, local papers, and even radio stations and cable television, are hungry for news, especially about local residents. Give them what they want on a regular basis. Keep them on your media list and they will repay you with more publicity and coverage than you could imagine or ever afford to buy.

Your media list is still not totally complete—it never will be—but you have developed a very usable list. Keep adding to the list, especially the names of trade and professional magazines and newsletters. Keep the list current, and if it is on your computer, make sure it is backed up on a disk. This could be one of your most important marketing possessions.

Invest in the paper and stamps to keep these people informed. You may even want to send releases to consumer-oriented national magazines in your field. All you need is a mention in one of these magazines and you are instantly perceived as an expert. Think what this does for your image.

ASK YOURSELF

► Describe the basic elements of a good press release.

► Why are press releases so popular with small business owners?

► Discuss the appropriate schedule for you to send out press releases.

► Elaborate on the steps for building your media list.

► Identify and outline other methods that you can use to complement your press release.

GROW YOUR BUSINESS THROUGH PERCEIVED EXPERTISE

BUILDING YOUR EXPERT BUSINESS IMAGE

Your small business is really no different from your competitors down the street or across town. You sell the same thing, provide similar levels of service, offer similar pricing schedules, and probably run similar types of ads. Somehow, you must begin to differentiate yourself from your competitors and assume a leadership or expert position in the minds of your customers and prospects.

These next several small business strategies and techniques will help you succeed, even where large corporations fail. Do not be fooled by these low cost no cost marketing tactics. The important thing to remember is that they work.

Businesses are made or broken by their images and reputations. This is more true in the small business arena than anywhere else. Remember that your image is how your customers, prospects and competitors see you. Your reputation is what these people say about you to others.

You need both a physical appearance image and a professional business image, as well as a positive reputation. If one of these is lacking, your business can easily fail. While you continue working on the physical image—the appearance of your facility, office and people—the following techniques will make you successful with your professional image and reputation.

Meet, Greet and Be Sweet

This is also known as shaking hands, patting backs and kissing babies. Before you say that it sounds too much like a politician's approach, be aware of how many people that politicians, and you, will meet this way. You have to go out and meet people. You have to get people to know you and your business. Introduce yourself to them. Tell them about your business. Better yet, ask them to tell you about what they do, and then tell them about what you do.

The more people you meet, greet and be sweet—nice, friendly, courteous, professional—to, the more opportunities you have to market your business. Remember, if someone you meet does not become a client or a customer immediately, they may do so at a later date, or they can always refer you to someone else or someone else to you. Therefore, view everyone you meet as a potential client/customer. Treat them with the highest respect.

Be a Joiner

Several years ago, I had a client who was an independent consultant. This person appeared to have everything going for him. He was educated, certified, presented an attractive and professional appearance and possessed excellent communication skills. Yet, his consulting business was going nowhere fast. The problem was very simple: This consultant knew he had all these positive attributes, so he felt they elevated him above the crowd and the competition. Therefore, clients would and should come to him. Right? Wrong.

As his business began to slide, I asked him to do two things. The first was to get rid of his "I'm better than everyone else" attitude and the unfounded expectation that customers would seek him out solely because of his credentials. The second thing I had him do was join several organizations. He agreed to speak to local business and professional groups for free.

He joined his local chamber of commerce, two local professional organizations, and a charity organization for which he became a volunteer committee member.

In three months, his consulting business tripled. All his new clients came from the organizations he joined and the speeches he gave to these organizations. His attitude also changed. Once a self-proclaimed loner, he now tells everyone to get involved with organizations.

No matter what you think of chambers of commerce or professional organizations, no matter how many people have told you that they never received one client from their memberships in these organizations, no matter how many people tell you they are a waste of your time and money, I am telling you now to waste your time and money. Join your local chamber of commerce and at least two professional organizations. Attend the meetings and offer to work on committees. Give presentations. Volunteer for a charity and work for them.

You may not receive any new business immediately, but you never know what the future will bring. In one month, three months, six months or even a year, someone from one of these organizations will refer themselves or another customer/client to you. Then, others will start to refer. What would you do if your entire customer base came from referrals from these association memberships? Would you turn them away? I do not think so.

People and companies have different motivations to buy small businesses' goods and services, and they have different buying cycles. You can assure yourself of being there for them when they are ready to purchase by being a member of their organizations and participating with them. Be around and be visible. Promote your business by asking them about theirs. The more they get to know you, the more they will like you—and the more they will eventually want to do business with you.

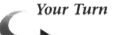

Your Turn   *Answer the following questions.*

▶ Describe the steps or techniques you have taken to create your business image and reputation.

▶ You already possess certain expertise. That is why you opened your small business. What are your strengths or areas of expertise?

▶ What have you done to date to communicate your expertise to the general public, your customers and your competitors?

FIVE GREAT WAYS TO CREATE AN EXPERT IMAGE AND REPUTATION

#1: Become Certified

Your entire image is based on how you are perceived by the public. If you are perceived as the expert in your business or field, people will come to you for advice and to do business.

The first way to create that image and the subsequent reputation of an expert is to become certified in something related to your business or field. Get additional training and a certificate of achievement. Go back to school to earn another degree. Then, send out a press release announcing that you have received this local, regional or national professional certification. This certification signifies that you have an extensive body of knowledge in your field and that you provide high quality service while maintaining the clients' best interests. Send out a press release each time you receive a new certification, complete additional training or receive a degree. People love initials and credentials. They will look to you as an expert because you have taken the time and made the effort to advance yourself to serve your customers better.

#2: Become a Local Resource for the Media

Now you can use your media contacts that you made while developing your media list. Telephone them or write to them and tell them you are available as a local resource for any questions they may have in your business or field. Whenever there is something in the news about small businesses in general, or your type of business in particular, write or call your media contacts and offer your opinion, recommendations and suggestions.

Eventually, someone in the media will ask you to give your views on a small business-related topic and will publicize your name and business. When you are mentioned or quoted in print or on the radio or television, you are automatically perceived by the public as an expert. This dramatically and instantaneously enhances your reputation and image. So, become a resource for the media.

#3: Publish and Flourish

You have to begin writing and publishing your views on subjects, your knowledge about your business or industry and any other information customers can use or that can influence them. Where you publish your information does not matter. What matters is that you publish.

Contact small, local newspapers and ask them if they want a column on small business, marketing, customer service, management, investments or whatever your small business area of expertise is. Offer to write the column for free, especially if they are interested in having you write on a regular basis.

The thing you want most from writing these articles is the byline and short biography at the end of the article telling about you and your business. Clip the article and use it as a publicity piece.

What do you do if no one will let you write for them? The answer is simple. Publish your own material. Write a pamphlet on training or operations techniques. Write a special report on a topic and make it available for purchase, or write a book. Then send a press release to the papers saying the pamphlet is available for free and the report or book can be purchased for a special price. When people respond, send the information to them with your business card. People believe what they read in print. Since you wrote the pamphlet, report or book, you must be an expert.

Take this concept a step further: Publish your own book, magazine or newsletter. It does not matter what your publication is, as long as it is a published work. Use the publication as a publicity piece to promote your business.

If you think it is difficult to publish your own book, think again. Several years ago, I was asked to present a marketing workshop for an international professional organization. No one in that organization had ever presented a three-hour marketing program before this one. Obviously, the turnout was going to be great, and it was even better than expected. Knowing I had a captive audience, I took the concept of producing handouts one step further and wrote a training manual on marketing their small business services. This self published manual was 90 pages, typewritten and photocopied; I sold it at the workshop for $20. More than 80 people paid me cash for that manual.

This gave me instant credibility as a marketing expert in this particular field. Even better, one year and 1,000 copy sales later, a major trade publishing house requested that I revise the manual so they could publish it as a hardcover book. I made the revisions, they published the book and I now had the image and reputation as the marketing expert in that field. As they say, the rest is history.

Here is one other story. A former client of mine mentioned that he had written a manuscript that he felt made a contribution to his particular field. Since he did not have anyone to publish it, I recommended he publish it himself, sell it at conferences and workshops, and then shop it around for a publisher. He followed my advice and later published his first book with a national publishing house. Now he is positioned as an expert in his field, and he is being asked to make presentations based on his book all over the country.

I tell you these stories to encourage you to write and publish your own materials. While you never know where it may lead, you can be certain that it will enhance your credibility, reputation and image as an expert in your field. Why do you think you are reading this book now? Because I already have credibility as a marketing expert from my previous books and articles. Moreover, this book adds to my credibility, reputation and image as a marketing consultant for small businesses. Again, I encourage you to write, publish and flourish.

#4: Tell It Like It Is

You have got to get your word out. The best way to do this is to give speeches to civic groups, community groups, professional organizations and charities. Let people know of your expertise. Get out there and tell them why and how they will benefit from being your customer.

Contact all the civic and professional organizations in your area. Offer your services as a speaker at one of their meetings to their program director. Everyone is interested in some aspect of small business success, especially when you are a local entrepreneur. If you get on their program, you have a built-in and captive audience. You just have to be able to get on their program.

I am often asked by business owners, consultants and entrepreneurs about charging a fee for speaking engagements. I recommend you do the following.

If you are just starting out, never charge. You should be thrilled that other professionals and community members want to hear what you have to say. Once you establish your track record, you can ask the organizations if they provide a speaker's honorarium. If they do, accept what they offer. If they do not, speak anyway, since you should not pass up the opportunity to meet and talk in front of new people.

After you become recognized as an expert and a "professional" speaker, you can start setting and requesting speaking fees. How much you request and how much you receive depends on your image and reputation in your field. Remember not to price yourself out of an engagement by being too costly. The more people hear you speak, the more speeches you will be offered, and the more potential clients/customers you will eventually have.

Do not confuse the small financial gain you may receive from a speech with the unmatched potential of future revenues from new business from the audience. Even though I can now ask for and receive a nice fee for speaking to companies and groups, I sometimes forego that fee for the potential future business that I will receive. Of course, I do my homework and evaluate that potential up front. If it is there, I am more than willing to adjust my fee, and sometimes forfeit it or donate it to charity, for the future business.

#5: Be Wise, Advise

People's perceptions of experts is that they advise, and this advice is usually accurate, good or profitable. Otherwise, why would they be considered experts? Since experts advise, try to get yourself on an advisory board.

This can be an advisory board to a company, a charity, a civic association or professional organization. When people learn that you are on an advisory board, they will instantly have respect for your expertise and want to do business with you rather than your competitors. This becomes even more true if the advisory board you are on has a credible reputation in the community.

You must be careful, though. Membership on advisory boards sometimes becomes addicting. Try not to overextend yourself by becoming a board member of numerous groups. Choose those boards which you can best serve and will provide you the greatest potential for increasing your business. If you spread yourself too thin, your "expertise" will deteriorate and your professional image and reputation will suffer.

Finally, be very careful about how you try to persuade other board members to do business with you. If you are too pushy, they will vote you off the board. Be courteous, friendly and informative without being overbearing; use this as an opportunity to network with other business owners and leaders. Eventually, business will come from your involvement.

OTHER IMAGE BUILDERS

Three other very important image builders should never be overlooked or taken for granted. They are your business card, your stationery, and you.

Your Business Card

Take a good look at your business card. Do you like it? Are you satisfied with it? How it looks? What it says? Does it portray the image you want it to portray? Does it send the message you intended it to send? If it does not, or if you are not sure, you need to change your business card immediately.

The business card is one of the least expensive and most important marketing tools you can use. Because of its importance and effectiveness, never skimp on a business card. Make certain it has all pertinent information such as your company or business name, address, telephone and fax numbers, your name and anything else you think must be on it.

However, do not clutter the card. If you do not have artistic or creative ability, pay an artist to design a logo and business card for you. This investment of a few hundred dollars will more than pay for itself as people perceive you have a high quality image because your business card is of high quality.

Have the card printed on good stock—at least 80 pound. If you know nothing about printing, check with your artist or graphic designer before your printer. Artists and printers are usually very good at helping you pick out a card stock and style that will help you portray your desired image.

Some people feel they need to have color on their cards. Color certainly calls attention to your business card and makes it stand out. If you need color to express your message, use it.

The photo business card is another type of card to consider. They are obviously very eye catching, but have one drawback: It sometimes is difficult to print over a color photo. Check with your local printer or supplier of these types of cards before you invest in them; they cost more than regular business cards, and I know of no research that indicates they create more business than regular black and white or color business cards.

Business cards are important because people expect you to have them and use them. The easiest way to give someone a business card is to ask them first for theirs. They will respond in kind, or accept yours as you offer it to them. You may even want to give them two cards, one for a friend—read referral.

If you have a storefront, make sure you have business cards at the cash register. You and your staff should give every customer a business card, whether they make a purchase or not. If they make a purchase, put the business card in the bag for them. People tend to keep business cards, especially if they are satisfied with their purchase and your service.

Your Letterhead

Your business cards are complemented by your letterhead. The logos and print styles on both the cards and stationery must be similar, and the quality of the letterhead must be equal to that of the business cards. Your envelopes should match your letterhead in content and quality, although it is not necessary to reprint your logo on the envelopes if it is on the letterhead. Be aware that printing envelopes costs more than printing letterhead. If an artist prepared your logo, business cards and letterhead, have that person design your envelopes. You must send a consistent image and message to customers and prospects.

This advice may seem simplistic. You might be surprised how many business professionals and small business owners do not pay enough attention to their business cards, letterheads and envelopes; the result is often lost business. No one in any small business can afford to lose a customer.

Always Look the Part

You have some great basic advice on how to create your expert image. In Chapter 6 we will discuss how to develop professional literature, such as brochures and fliers, that will further enhance your image and reputation. For now, focus on creating the packaging that goes along with your business—that packaging is you and your people.

You must look and live the part of the small business owner or professional—well groomed, polite, attentive and physically and mentally prepared to meet the daily challenges of your job. Your appearance is your packaging. This is especially true for consultants, physicians, attorneys, accountants and other service professionals.

Another important aspect of looking the part is matching your appearance to the client or customer you are trying to secure or work with. For example, if you are selling casual wear clothing in a small, rural town, you probably do not want to come to work in a three-piece suit. If you are selling high fashion clothing, you definitely do not want to look like you just returned from a football game. Look the part and have the image the customer expects.

Likewise, if you are approaching a country club to sell them golf or tennis equipment or professional services and the club manager or pro suggests you come dressed casually, make certain you dress in that manner. Showing up in an expensive suit to walk around the golf course will not get you the customer you want.

The more you match your appearance to that of your clients and prospects and, perhaps more importantly, match their expectations of what you should look like, the better your chances are of securing more business. In addition, your clients and customers will now market for you, making referrals and enhancing your reputation; they like you and perceive that you are like them. Do you know of a better, more effective and less expensive marketing technique than referrals and word-of-mouth?

ASK YOURSELF

► Which of the five techniques for creating expertise and improving your image and reputation do you already use? Discuss the ones you will start using immediately.

► Review your business cards, stationery and personal appearance, as well as the appearance of your employees. Describe the results of your review.

► Identify the steps you will take on a regular basis to continue to upgrade your image and reputation in the community.

CHAPTER
FOUR

SIMPLE AND
POWERFUL
PUBLIC RELATIONS
STRATEGIES

GOOD PUBLIC RELATIONS

Many so-called experts think they know exactly what public relations is and are only too glad to tell you. Be careful. Some of these experts tell you that public relations costs nothing. Wrong. Other experts tell you that public relations is sending out press releases and waiting for the media to pick them up. Wrong again. Still others say that public relations is any coverage or publicity that is provided for you by a third party. This is a narrow view of public relations—expect more from your PR efforts.

Much more than any or all of these things, PR is the total of all your work and efforts that results in publicity for you and your business. PR may be free, but more often than not costs are associated with it. These costs include time, personnel, effort, paper, postage, telephone calls, materials, travel and everything else that you put into getting that large or small dose of publicity.

First I will give you an example of good public relations; then I will tell you how to develop your effective PR campaign. A client of mine, a small yogurt store, was about to open in a highly competitive urban area. Unlike their mega-chain competitors, they did not have an extensive marketing or advertising budget. In fact, they had almost no budget. And, the owner did not know much about how to generate publicity. What the store did have was healthy and delicious yogurt products. It was my job to let the public know about them.

First, I convinced the owner to have a "soft" opening. A soft opening is when you open the store with a minimum of advertising, fanfare and publicity. Your goal is to "get the kinks out," get your systems in place, and make certain your staff is trained. I had them stay "soft" for sixty days, which gave us enough time to plan their grand opening.

They had budget of $400 for the grand opening. This is so minimal for a grand opening that I recommended the store donate the entire amount to a local charity. I contacted the owner's favorite charity and told them the date and time of the donation and asked them to send a representative to the opening. I called newspaper editors and assignment editors at radio and television stations with the same information. I emphasized the charity donation. This was the "hook" to get the media involved. People love charities.

After the telephone calls, I sent a letter about the event and upcoming public donation to the media contacts. The letter confirmed the telephone call and reminded these people they were invited to attend the grand opening and cover the story.

Three weeks, two weeks and one week before the event, I sent press releases to all the media about the grand opening. I also called them to make certain they received the releases. I wanted to be sure the media knew the opening was going to happen. I found a local talk radio station that had a health-related show on it. I convinced the hosts to hold their show "live" from the store on that day. They mentioned their remote broadcast for several weeks before the event, which increased the turnout.

Since the owner provided me with no money to advertise, I had to do something to inform the rest of the public. I "traded out" advertising time with several radio stations for free yogurt. While there may be a way to equate costs associated with a tradeout of this type, there really is no way to place a price on the value the yogurt store received from the "free" radio advertising. Because more than one station aired the commercials, which were actually public service announcements (PSAs) about the grand opening and charity donation, the public perceived that this was a well-financed community-oriented operation.

The grand opening was a tremendous success. More than 300 people visited the store during the six hours of the grand opening; 30% of the people who came that day became regular customers. I tracked their repeat purchases through frequent buyer cards. The total cost to the store was the $400 the owners donated to the charity, which was tax deductible, plus a small outlay for paper and postage.

A Review of the Public Relations for the Event

Let us quickly review the public relations activities that were conducted for this event. First, there was a charity tie-in. The media love to cover charity events and donations to charities. The incremental exposure from this alone was worth more than $20,000. Next, letters, telephone calls and press releases were sent, and more telephone calls were made to the media about the charity donation at the grand opening. This led to additional coverage. Third, a local radio talk show conducted their show live from the store, which led to even more free promotion. Fourth, free advertising was received through tradeouts. Finally, once the grand opening was over, I sent out a press release telling everyone about the tremendously successful event.

Can You Apply These Techniques to Your Small Business?

The answer is a definite yes. Adapt them, modify them or follow them exactly as they are presented here for any event you want to hold at your store, office or place of business. They have worked for me and my clients in more than 50 industries, and they will definitely work for you. Of course, these strategies are not the only public relations techniques you can use, as you will learn throughout this chapter.

GOALS AND OBJECTIVES OF PUBLIC RELATIONS

The primary goal of public relations is to get media coverage for your business, preferably at little or no cost. Another goal is to create and enhance your public image and business reputation. A third objective is to create and sustain community goodwill and positive community relations. Following are some ways to generate that publicity, further build that positive image and maintain that reputation and community goodwill.

Press Releases

Press releases are the most common method for informing the media and the public about what you are doing. While there truly is no right or wrong way to write a release, most editors are used to seeing them in one or two standard formats. To be on the safe side, refer to Chapter 2 and the material below to see how to write a press release for your small business.

Many topics can command attention, but you can be sure that editors will always be partial to human interest stories. What has your business done to help someone in need? How have you improved the quality of life in your community for one person or a group of people?

Ask your employees for ideas in this area. Maybe you can do a press release on something one of your employees did to help a customer. Perhaps someone in your business went out of their way to make sure a customer was satisfied. If so, tell everyone about it. When people read about it in the paper, or hear about it, they will probably come to your store to shop or to meet the "hero."

Here are some important review points about generating your news release: Highlight and/or capitalize the title of the release, skip two lines and put the city and state associated with the release. Then begin your message. Double space between lines so the piece is easy to read, and the editor can make any changes necessary for publication. Write your release from the specific to the general; answer the questions who, what, when, where, how and why right at the beginning of the release. Remember, editors cut from the bottom up; write your most important information at the beginning of the release. (See the sample press release that follows.)

Keep the press release to one or two pages. The entire release needs to keep the editor's interest and constantly provide information or he or she will stop reading. Then your chances of publicity are zero.

Remember, too, that your press release is one of many the media receive. Be creative and make it stand out from the crowd. Use the article approach, or include some graphics. Or, reverse out the headline and use white print on a black background. Whatever you do, be creative.

NEWS RELEASE

DATE: Today's Date

CONTACT: Richard F. Gerson

TELEPHONE: (xxx) xxx-xxxx

FOR IMMEDIATE RELEASE

NEW BOOK TELLS BUSINESSES HOW TO EXCEED CUSTOMER SERVICE AND SATISFY CUSTOMERS

Safety Harbor, Florida—With everybody using the business buzzwords of quality improvement and customer service, it is no longer enough to offer these to customers and hope to be successful and profitable in this decade and beyond. Businesses need to exceed customer service and work to satisfy and retain their customers, says Dr. Richard Gerson, author of the new book, *Beyond Customer Service.* Only when your business can offer your customers something of additional value, establish a long-term relationship with them and provide them with reasons for remaining loyal to you, can you hope to be profitable, adds Dr. Gerson.

-MORE-

The keys to business success today are 100% customer satisfaction, long-term customer retention, and the development of customer referral networks as marketing tools. Gerson's book teaches business owners how to achieve all these things through well-written, concise tips and techniques. Using tables, charts and lists, the book describes how everyone can go beyond customer service to achieve customer satisfaction, improve their service quality and then develop marketing programs around these approaches.

The book also describes how to develop and implement a customer service system, how to train your employees to provide superior customer service, how to add value to your business and help satisfy your customers and suggests 50 ways to serve and satisfy everyone you do business with. Tables, charts and forms to fill in help you learn more about what your customers need, want and expect from you.

The book, along with Dr. Gerson's *Writing and Implementing a Marketing Plan,* is published by Crisp Publications of Menlo Park, California.

###

Charities

Every small business should be associated with a local charity or a local chapter of a national organization. The publicity you receive from this alliance is tremendous. You can publicize it, and the charity will definitely publicize it. Hold fundraisers for the charity, do special events, volunteer for their committees and boards, and host open houses for their volunteers and paid staff. Do anything and everything you can for a charity—the media will love you. More importantly, the buying public will love you and continue to do business with you.

Other Publicity Opportunities

One of the purposes of public relations is to create a perception of you as an expert, or your store as the place to shop, either because of your quality, prices, service or all three. You need to put yourself in the public's eye constantly and reinforce all the wonderful things you can do for the community at your place of business. Choose from among the following ideas to create your image as a credible expert while generating publicity for your business.

Publish

Write articles. It is as simple as that. Call your local weekly newspaper or some other publication and offer to write articles for them. You do not have to be paid for writing. All you want is a byline and a brief biography about you and your business at the end of the article. If you have one, send a picture to the publication. The more articles you write, the more the public will see your name and face; they will start to consider you an expert.

You can also write for trade publications. Find out what they are, contact the editors, tell them who you are and your qualifications and describe the article you want to write. To determine their level of interest, write a query—inquiry—letter with an outline of your article. You can also write the article first, send it unsolicited, and hope they will print it.

How powerful is this publicity technique of publishing articles? It works for me: I have published more than 200 articles in both professional and popular publications. I was paid for some of the articles, and I wrote some of them for free. I also used the articles as a tradeout for advertising. My purpose was to generate publicity, create an image and reputation and position myself as an expert. I also wanted to compile a selection of articles for my press kit and as mailers to prospects and clients, to enhance my credibility and position as an expert.

It seems to have worked. I receive telephone requests from people all over the country to speak to companies and groups and to consult. I know many of these leads come from my articles, because I ask callers where they got my number or heard of me.

Remember that people believe what they see in print. The more articles you publish related to your business or industry, the more of an expert the public will perceive you to be. Also, you can write your own book or booklet. Self-publish it, and send out press releases announcing it. Self-publishing has achieved a level of credibility now that it never had before. As long as the information you are publishing is timely and helpful, you can tell the world you have written and published a book.

In today's computerized world of desktop publishing, writing and publishing a book is not that difficult. Here are five easy steps for you to follow to publish your own book:

1. Select a topic with which you are very familiar.

2. Create an outline of chapter headings to serve as a guide.

3. Write out a summary of each chapter before writing the entire chapter.

4. Write the manuscript expanding the summaries into chapters. If you write only a page a day for a year, you will have a 365-page book which, when printed, will be more than 200 pages.

5. Select a printer who will work with you to print and bind the book. If your laser printer is good enough, find someone to reproduce your originals and bind them. Now, you have a book. That was not so hard, was it?

Here is another suggestion. Let us say you do not have the time or motivation to write a book right now. How about writing five-, 10- or 20-page "special reports." These special reports focus on an aspect of your business that other people would be interested in. For example, write a special report on how customers can receive the most value for their money, how you have trained your employees to provide superior service, how you use customer feedback to improve your service systems or how your employee incentives increase your sales by 20% over the industry average.

You get the idea. Then, when you have written seven or eight special reports, you have almost enough material for a book. You can sell those special reports to competitors, interested readers, and even to your customers. It is like getting paid in advance to write a book you have always dreamed about.

Here is another simple way to publish something. Let us assume you provide excellent customer service in your business, and you train your staff in these techniques. Just write down the methods you use to train them, bullet point them, and call the booklet *Ten Tips to Superior Customer Service*. You might even want to sell it to your competitors, but do not do that until after you have sufficiently publicized your booklet in the media.

Let me tell you something personal. My consulting practice was very successful using many of the marketing strategies I teach in this book. However, my practice did not start booming until I used my first business marketing book, *Writing and Implementing a Marketing Plan* published by Crisp Publications, as a living brochure. This became my best marketing tool. Combined with my next Crisp Publications books, *Beyond Customer Service* and *Measuring Customer Satisfaction*, I had a triple-barreled approach to marketing. Prospects and customers loved it, and even if I did not turn every prospect into a customer after my presentation, many prospects bought both books for their personal libraries. The credibility power of your name on a published book is unbelievable.

Think seriously about publishing articles, special reports and books.

Your Turn

Answer the following:

► Have you ever written anything for publication? An article, a booklet or a book? How about a training manual for your employees?

► Have you ever given a speech? Any kind of speech will do. How about a talk to your staff on some aspect of the business? Tape record your presentation and have it transcribed. Now you have a publishable training manual.

► What other strategies, tactics and techniques can you use to publish something to enhance your credibility and improve your image and reputation?

Speak

Give speeches. Talk whenever you can at lunch club meetings. Try to speak at trade meetings and conventions. Give as many speeches as you can, especially when you are just starting.

Use your speaking abilities in another way. Speak out on issues related to small business in general, and your area of it in particular. Become a media resource. Contact media people; let them know, should they have any questions, you are available as an expert in the field.

Get interviewed. Call up local talk show hosts and offer to be a guest on their show. Talk about a timely topic and always mention your business. These shows can be on network affiliates, cable TV or radio. When customers see you on TV or hear you on the radio, they will automatically perceive you as an expert and strongly consider doing business with you.

Seminars and Workshops

These are natural extensions of your speaking engagements. Offer seminars to your customers on how they can do something better. If your small business relies on referrals from others, offer seminars to the referral sources. Remember to make the topic timely and beneficial to the participants. Try not to sell too much during the seminar. The fact that you are hosting the program will start the sales message playing in their minds.

Your goal with seminars and workshops is to get people familiar with you and your business, so that they will buy from you or refer to you. If possible, do not charge for these programs. Once you have a reputation in your industry, you can start charging for the programs.

If your store, office or facility is large enough, hold the seminar at your place of business. Get customers familiar with your location so they feel comfortable coming to you. If you do not have a large enough facility or you work out of your home, hold the seminar in a convenient room or hall.

You can also conduct private seminars for corporations; then they are responsible for providing the location.

Speeches, seminars and workshops are great marketing strategies for you to gain publicity and improve your public relations.

Awards

If you get an award or a certification, publicize it. Better yet, give an award and publicize that. The media loves to cover award ceremonies. Give out awards for best employee and best customer or client in your store or office. Publicize these events. The more you are mentioned in a newspaper, or anywhere else, as being associated with someone else receiving an award, the greater your prospects are for gaining goodwill business.

New Hires and Promotions

Whenever you hire or promote someone, send a press release and their picture to the newspapers, telling who the person is, what they have done and what they will be doing for you. Make sure you mention your company name in the press release and where you can be reached.

This is an innocuous way of getting coverage; the newspapers are only too happy to print good news about other people. Also, send them information on your own personal good news events.

Your Press/Publicity Kit

It may seem that many small businesses have their own brochure, when in fact, most of them do not. For those that use brochures, most of them are "me" pieces, rather than sales pieces. Me brochures tell about the company or business without telling readers why it is beneficial for them to do business with that company. That is why so many brochures are thrown away. Readers see no benefit from the brochure, since it never involves them. Instead of a brochure, think about developing a press or publicity kit—capabilities presentation—for yourself and your business.

The press kit is much more effective than any type of brochure, and the kit makes a greater impact on prospects and customers.

Your press kit can be a folder-type binder with slip pockets and a slot for your business card; it can even be a three-ring binder. If you use a three-ring binder to make presentations, make certain all the pages are in vinyl sheets. This protects the pages from tearing when you turn them. During a sales presentation, the binder makes a strong impact on the prospect or customer. Furthermore, if they request it, I mail them or drop off a folder-type press kit with the material. This gives me another contact with the prospect—another chance to get my name in front of them.

Here are some suggestions about the content of your press kit or presentation binder. You can decide what you will send to customers, or ask them what they want as reminder information from your binder.

▶ *Company Description*—This is a one- or two-page description of your company, its history, the programs and services it offers, its customer service philosophy and its approaches to helping customers. Keep this description positive and upbeat and try to involve the reader.

▶ *Personal Biography*—As the owner or marketing contact for your company, people want to know with whom they are dealing. Provide information on who you are, your background and achievements and how you will help your customers.

▶ *Client List*—Provide a list of your clients or people you have done business with. For example, if you are a professional consultant or distributor, you may want to list corporations that you have served or who have participated in your programs.

▶ *Client Benefits*—Always sell benefits, then support these with the features. List all the benefits your customers will receive from working with you or buying from you.

▶ *Testimonial Letters*—The more testimonial letters that sing your praises you can provide, the higher your credibility and the more people who will perceive you as an expert. While this is especially important for individual service providers and professionals, it is also vitally important for store owners. Customers should come in and see letters from satisfied customers posted on a bulletin board or contained neatly in a binder on a table or on the counter. These letters enhance your credibility, image and reputation and make new customers want to continue to do business with you.

▶ *Program Descriptions*—Describe the programs and services you offer, if this is the nature of your business. If you teach seminars and workshops, write an outline of these programs and include a list of benefits that people will receive from participating in your programs.

▶ *Publications*—Provide samples or reprints of any articles you wrote. People enjoy doing business with published authors. Also, provide reprints of articles that have been written by other authors about you. Both of these strategies enhance your credibility.

These are the contents of a press kit or, at least, the contents of the one I use. Include your business card, black and white photos of yourself, and any other information about your business that you feel is important. Press kits can accompany press releases or requests for more information about you or your company. They can also be sent with business proposals—consultants, take note. In any case, the press kit must sell you to the readers for you to gain publicity, an awareness in their minds and, eventually, more business.

Sponsorships

Another great public relations opportunity, and an excellent marketing tool, is a sponsorship of a local athletic team, youth group, senior group or special event. Although this may cost you some money, the return on your investment is tremendous. You build community goodwill and get your name in front of the public.

You can sponsor Little League baseball teams, soccer teams, high school athletic events, community dances, fund raisers, special trips or outings, a Cub/Girl Scout troop, charity events, races, aerobic dance marathons, disaster relief efforts, scholarships and anything else you can think of. The key is to sponsor something and publicize it so everyone knows of your efforts on the community's behalf.

CULTIVATING PUBLIC RELATIONS

People often wonder why their press releases do not get printed, their event announcements do not receive any coverage, and the media seems uninterested in what they are doing. It is usually not because your event or news release is without merit, although if it is, you need to review the material you are sending and re-evaluate its newsworthiness.

Remember, media people always have a full plate; your press release must be extremely newsworthy to get through to them and warrant coverage. Here is how to increase your chances of getting media coverage.

Take an editor to lunch. This is true. Call up your local newspaper editor, news director, assignment editor, or whoever has the authority to decide whether or not you will receive media coverage. Say that you want to meet personally to introduce yourself and would like to do this over lunch—or breakfast or dinner. If they refuse, ask if you can come to their office to meet and to drop off some material about you or your business that might be of interest.

Keep in regular contact. When you have something newsworthy, call and offer an exclusive on your event. If you offer an exclusive, never provide the information to another medium until your first one has either covered it or rejected it. Or, just call them up to see how they are doing. People appreciate not being sold all the time.

When you get coverage, send letters thanking the editor for that coverage. Send items of interest from your field, such as excerpts from trade journals or business magazines. Keep in touch, even when you do not have anything newsworthy for them. In fact, this may get you more coverage because they will perceive that every time they hear from you, it is not just for publicity. If you cannot become their friend, at least be friendly.

Put Yourself on a Schedule

One more thing about public relations and publicity—put yourself on a regular schedule for the year to inform the media and public about your newsworthy accomplishments or events. This can be monthly, quarterly, or even bi-annually. Make sure you stick to this schedule and that the material you send in, or the events you sponsor or host, are newsworthy enough to warrant free media coverage.

Remember that sending out press releases involves postage costs, so be judicious with what you mail. Mass mailing to all types of media in hope of getting publicity is nothing more than a fruitless, expensive and foolish exercise.

Target your media markets as carefully as you target your customer markets. Nurture them in the same way you do customers, to grow your publicity efforts to where the media is glad to hear from you. Then, publicize, publicize, publicize, and keep all the above principles in mind.

ITEMS TO PUBLICIZE

Here are the 10 areas that editors of newspapers and magazines and assignment editors at television and radio stations find the most interesting. If your release addresses one of these areas, you have a much better chance of receiving publicity.

1. *Newsworthy*—Make sure your release covers something newsworthy. A new invention, a new way to do something and a new approach to customer service would all be newsworthy, as would relating your work to something that is getting daily coverage in the news.

2. *"How To" Information*—People love to read useful advice. If you can tell readers how to save money on taxes, repair their homes inexpensively or market their businesses effectively and at little or no cost, you will get your release published.

3. *Interesting Information*—Facts and survey results fascinate both editors and readers. If you have completed a survey of customer interests, publish the results in a release. Who knows, you may get a full-fledged article out of it.

4. *Human Interest*—People love to read about other people, especially when it is good news. What have you or your people accomplished? What has your business done to help someone in your community? What are you doing for the environment, to stop crime or feed starving children? You get the idea. Now, write something about it.

5. *Controversy*—Take an opposite viewpoint from an expert or columnist. Point out a possible controversy that exists in your industry. Do not target a specific competitor. Be general. Controversy arouses people's interest and creates allegiances, especially when you are promoting the "good guy" side of the controversy.

6. *Timeliness*—What are you doing that fits right in with what is going on in the world or your community? Make a statement about a newsworthy event and show how your business is working to improve on that event.

7. *Stars*—Has someone in your business done something to achieve their 15 minutes of fame? Let everybody know about it. People love to see their name in print, and people like to publish stories about local and national stars. Receiving awards also fits in well here.

8. *Special Events*—Any type of special event, such as a grand opening, or an expansion, deserves publicity. Let the public know about your event. Time and space permitting, the media enjoys publicizing special events.

9. *Charitable Acts*—Do you give away food, clothing or lodging at any time during the year, especially around the holidays? Have you made a donation to one or more charities? Does your staff do volunteer work for charities and civic organizations? Do you provide a scholarship for a deserving student? These are just some of the charitable acts that will get you tremendous publicity.

10. *Success Stories*—Everyone likes to read about other people's successes. It gives the reader "warm fuzzies" and makes the subject feel great. Your chances of publicity with success stories increase dramatically when the success is the result of overcoming hardship, a rags-to-riches story or a major achievement in the face of seemingly insurmountable odds. Other success stories, such as a graduation, certification or receipt of an award, will also generate publicity.

Over the years, these ten areas have proven to receive the most publicity for me and my clients. If you check other resources, you will find that they, too, recommend some or all of these areas as having the greatest potential for coverage. Try to think of variations of these "hot" topics. Use them to get publicity for your small business. Come up with additional areas of interest. How? Ask your editors. They will tell you what they want from you.

You now have an extensive arsenal of marketing strategies that will help you get the publicity your business needs. Figure out how to package them to suit your needs best and go out and make them work for you. If you do not, you can be sure your competitors will.

ASK YOURSELF

► Discuss the public relations strategies and techniques mentioned in this chapter that you use.

  • Which are the most effective and why?

► Describe your successes in getting media coverage.

  • What topics are getting that media coverage for you?

► Describe how you can use each of the public relations techniques mentioned in this chapter to gain more publicity for your business.

CHAPTER
FIVE

ADVANCED
PUBLIC
RELATIONS
TECHNIQUES

GETTING THEIR ATTENTION

Sometimes sending a press release or calling a media contact is not enough. You have to do more to get their attention and convince them that the material you have sent warrants publication or mention on a news show. Here are several simple, effective and successful techniques you can use to grab the attention of the media.

THE PRESS RELEASE ARTICLE

Media people receive many press releases from all types of businesses. Sometimes they get so many releases that they do not even read them. Most of these releases look alike. Therefore, you must make your release stand out from the crowd.

One way is to make your press release look innovative and attractive to the reader and easier for the editor to print or the assignment editor to give to an announcer. I use something I call the press release article. I print my press releases in a two-column format that resembles a newspaper article. I even write a heading like a newspaper article. This heading can be straight black print on white paper or it can be reversed out—the choice is yours.

I have two reasons for using the press release article instead of the traditional press release. First, the different format makes it stand out. Most people do not send a press release with a bold, glaring headline that captures the reader's attention. Nor do they usually send one in an article format. When you do this, the information about your small business stands out.

The second reason is that a press release in article format has a good chance of getting printed as an article by a newspaper or magazine. They do not have to rewrite it nor do they have to reformat it. They simply have to typeset it and print it. So, if you are a good writer, put your skills to work and send your press releases in article format. Again, keep the length to one or two pages.

The sample on the following page shows you exactly what this type of article press release looks like. When you send these to newsletter publishers, they tend to publish them because the article is already written. That gives you another marketing outlet for your information and builds your image and reputation as an expert and someone people should do business with.

Your Turn

Modify a press release that you have previously sent to your local media, or use the one you wrote for the practice exercise in Chapter 2 so it becomes an article press release.

► Do you have to change any of the formatting? What about the conventional symbols? Is there anything else you must change?

► Can you include a picture in your article press release? If you do not have the capabilities of scanning in a picture, mark the space for the picture on the release and provide the picture to the newspaper. If they use your release, they will place the picture for you.

BACKGROUNDERS

There are times when you cannot tell your whole story in a traditional press release or in the article format. You have too much to say to the public. In this case, write a backgrounder to supplement your press release.

Use either format for the press release, then write an extensive background piece detailing everything you want your reader to know about your small business. There is no specified or required length for the backgrounder. There is also no particular format you must follow, except that you should put a title on the piece, date it and clearly identify it as a backgrounder.

Marketing doctor makes sick businesses well!

It's no secret that there is an epidemic going around in business today. Record numbers of companies are sick and dying. Major employers, such as IBM, American Express and GE, who were once thought invincible are laying off employees and selling subsidiaries just to stay alive.

Businesses are hemorrhaging and they don't know how to stop the bleeding.

Tampa Bay is also not immune to this epidemic. The area is among the nation's leaders in bankruptcies and failed businesses. What is causing all this sickness?

The answer is poor marketing. Regardless of the economy, companies that do proper marketing can survive and thrive. Now, there is help for those companies that are sick, and those that are getting ill butdon't know it yet.

Dr. Richard Gerson, CMC, president of Gerson Goodson, Inc., is the marketing doctor. He works with businesses the same way a family physician works with an individual patient.

Businesses that are ill can call the marketing doctor at 726-7619. They will go through a process of assessment, evaluation, diagnosis and prescription very similar to that which their personal physician would follow. Then, a treatment program will be prescribed for the business to make it well.

A business that is ill, or having problems, or on the verge of closing, should call the marketing doctor to determine if its symptoms are curable. Then, Dr. Gerson will have the "patient" business complete a "health history and symptom analysis" questionnaire prior to the meeting. A diagnosis will be made and a treatment program (marketing/management recommendations) will be provided. The "patient" will complete the treatment program and then have a follow-up visit.

And, best of all, unlike today's medical physicians, the marketing doctor makes "house" (office) calls. Dr. Gerson will go directly to the patient's office or location to conduct the examination and prescribe the treatment.

The fee for each office visit is only $50, and that includes the health history, examination, diagnosis and treatment prescription. The follow-up visit is only $35.

Dr. Gerson is well qualified as the marketing doctor, and he has a long history of making businesses well. He is also the author of 11 books, 6 on marketing and 2 on customer service. He has made presentations to numerous corporate organizations and professional meetings on a state, regional and national level. He is recognized as an authority on marketing and considered one of the premier marketing consultants in the country.

For more information on theservices of the marketing doctor, call Dr. Gerson at 726-7619 or write to him at P.O. Box 1534, Safety Harbor, Fl., 34695.

The backgrounder ensures you cover all the information you feel must be covered to give the reader a complete and clear picture of your business or achievement. The media person reading the release and the backgrounder determines what he or she finds interesting and usable. You are better off being comprehensive and letting them edit your backgrounder or calling you to discuss it, rather than being tentative with the information.

Another benefit of sending a backgrounder is that it may supply enough supplemental and complementary information to your press release that the media will do a story on your business from the information you supplied. If you are presenting the backgrounder in an article format, they may print it exactly as you send it. Make certain the backgrounder supports the press release and they are both newsworthy.

DIRECT RESPONSE PRESS RELEASES

Here is an innovative idea for you. Most companies send a press release, hope the media publish it and wait for people to call. The following strategies are to get people to call you from your press release.

One way is to write a press release alerting your industry to certain things such as potential pitfalls in their business practices or a controversy that may arise. Write the release from a third party perspective. Tell the readers they can call your company for more information on this position.

Editors frequently publish this type of release because it is not self-serving. It appears to be altruistic in that you are trying to help your industry avoid possible problems. You may even get a call from the editor asking to do an in-depth story on your release.

Another direct response press release strategy is to make a statement in the release and offer a free information booklet. Tie the release to the information in the booklet. You may even want to reprint part of the booklet—one or two tips or suggestions—in the release. Then, tell the reader where to write or call for the booklet.

Editors like this approach for two reasons. First, they can run short blurbs on your material and offer their readers something for free. This creates a perception of added value in the minds of the readers toward the publication. The second reason is that they may be able to reprint some or all of your booklet as an article. Then, you are doubling the effectiveness of your press release.

The key to success with direct response press releases is to tell the reader what they must do next. Help them take the next step, which is either to call you or write you or come to your store for more information. If you do not tell them what to do and how to do it, they may not respond. It is up to you to get them to take action.

TEASERS

Teasers are press releases, or mini letters to the editor that do not tell the entire story. People or businesses who send teasers are hoping that the editor will become sufficiently interested in the topic, based on a minimal amount of information. These people may also be afraid to give away the store too soon.

My experience is that you should always tell the truth, the whole truth and nothing but the truth all the time when you communicate with the media. Do not send teaser releases. If you want to increase your chances of having a press release published, and you want your image and reputation to remain positive with the media, send them the entire story whenever you send a press release.

If you have doubts about this position, remember how you felt as a child when people teased you about something. Do not tease the media.

Now that you know what to send, you have to figure out where to send the information. You need a media list.

DEVELOPING YOUR MEDIA LIST

Do not buy a media list. I must emphasize this strongly and repeatedly. New business owners, whether they are small businesses, consultants, professionals or in other fields, tend to want the quickest route to contacting the media. Buying or renting a media list is definitely not the best way to make these contacts.

The media list you buy or rent can be outdated. Editors, assignment people, reporters and other possible contacts at a newspaper or radio or television station change jobs, locations and responsibilities all the time. They do not send out notices to small businesses to let them know they no longer receive press releases or other information.

You miss a great marketing opportunity when you buy a media list, rather than build and develop your own. Developing a media list is very simple, even if it is sometimes tedious. The development process is a great marketing and public relations opportunity for you. When you prepare your own media list, you make contacts with all the people who will eventually receive the information you will mail out. Build your media list by doing the following.

Open your *Yellow Pages* to the sections on newspapers, radio stations, television stations, associations and organizations. Copy down each business name, address and telephone number. This will be easiest if you have a computer and a database program, but it can be done by hand.

Once you have copied down or typed all the pertinent information, call each business, introduce yourself and your business and ask who receives press releases. You will usually get the name of the person and their title. If you get connected to that person, introduce yourself and your business and ask when and how often he or she likes to receive press releases, and what types of press releases they prefer. Ask this contact what they consider newsworthy in your industry. This information will help you hit their hot button when you send them a release.

Sometimes, media companies have specific people who work in particular industries, such as a consumer editor, a medical writer or a customer advocate. If your local newspaper, radio or TV stations has someone who specializes in small businesses, contact them directly. Introduce yourself and ask the appropriate questions. Then send them your press releases at the times they like to receive them. These times will usually either coincide with their deadlines or be in-between deadlines so they will have the chance to review your materials.

The Importance of Your Media List

This is probably the second most important list you will ever own and maintain. The first, of course, is your customer list. These people who have purchased from you before, or who have shown an interest in buying from you, are your bread and butter. After them, your media contacts can be vitally important to the success of your business. Your accurate and up-to-date media list becomes your link to these people and to the rest of the community.

Never underestimate or take for granted your media list or your media contacts.

WORD-OF-MOUTH MARKETING

Do you remember the old shampoo commercial in which a woman tells two friends, who tell two friends, who tell two friends, and so on? The power of word-of-mouth marketing multiplies geometrically and exponentially, whether it is good or bad.

Did you like that last restaurant where you ate? Did you dislike it? What did you tell your friends and family about it? Would you recommend it to them? Are you going back?

Your answers to these questions are all part of a word-of-mouth marketing program that will affect the success of that restaurant. Word-of-mouth marketing is also known as referrals and networking. Because word-of-mouth can be positive or negative, and referrals and networking are perceived positively, we will combine all the terms under word-of-mouth marketing.

Your Turn

Answer the following:

- ► Think of a recent good experience you had with a service provider. How many people did you tell?

- ► Think of a less than satisfactory experience you have had with a service provider. How many people did you tell?

- ► Think of a great experience with a service provider that someone told you about. What have you told other people about that business? Are you likely to go there?

- ► Think of a less than satisfactory experience with a service provider that someone told you about. What have you told other people about that business? Are you likely to go there?

Think back to your restaurant experience, or any experience you have had purchasing a product or receiving a service. If it was enjoyable and met your expectations, you were probably satisfied. And you may have told a few people about it. However, if you were unhappy with the purchase or experience, you probably told a few more people about how bad it was. This is the power of word-of-mouth marketing. Negative word-of-mouth can be four to five times more powerful than positive word-of-mouth. Therefore, do everything you can to develop a positive word-of-mouth marketing program.

Your Word-of-Mouth Marketing Program

People believe incorrectly they cannot control a word-of-mouth marketing program, but speeches, charities, sponsorships, publications, committees and other credibility builders spread the good word about your small business. As much as possible, you need to control this talk factor in a planned and prescribed manner.

Your word-of-mouth marketing program begins with the product or service you are selling. It must be of high quality and have a high perceived value by customers. It must also satisfy one of their needs or wants. Otherwise, it will be difficult for you to generate positive word-of-mouth.

Once you know what product or service you will sell, determine the message you want to communicate to the public about it. This message must tell customers the benefits they will receive from buying from you. Then you must get the message to the people.

The first way to get the message out is to listen to what is coming in. Meet and talk with your customers and clients. Walk around and talk to your employees. Listen to what they are telling you. What do they say about you and your business? Is what they say good or bad? What should you be paying more attention to? What must you do to improve in the areas they are talking about?

Review your customer records. See how many new customers are the result of referrals from clients? If your customer list is not at least 80% referral-based by your third year, identify what you are doing that is not attracting this business. This is critical for consultants and other service providers. Why do some people refer to you while others do not? What reasons do new customers have for becoming your clients or buying from you? Pay strict attention to the communications between customers, between employees and between customers and employees. This will provide you with invaluable information about your business, its chances for continued growth and success and the effectiveness of your overall marketing program.

Where to Begin

Begin your word-of-mouth marketing program internally, with your employees. If you are a sole practitioner, begin with yourself. Program yourself for positive comments and attitudes about your business. If you have employees, work with and train them so that they know more than just their jobs. They should know everything about your business, inside and outside. Share your knowledge and information with them, even what was once considered proprietary information. The more your employees know about your business, the more they can do to promote it.

Show your employees that you live the mission of your business. Let them see and experience your positive attitude so that they, in turn, can develop the same attitude and commitment. Train them, nurture them and reward them for their behaviors. Teach them what to say to whom, and when to say it. Empower them to make decisions to help the customers and let them insert their own personalities into their jobs. This will motivate employees to have the proper attitude about your business and to promote it to the community.

It is important to have all employees speaking positively about your business. You will usually find one or two employees who stand out above the rest. They are your champions. Work with them to make them even more of your marketing mouthpieces, to get the word out. Have them speak before community and professional groups and sit on committees. Make them an integral part of your business and marketing. You will be rewarded with a successful small business.

One other note about beginning your word-of-mouth marketing program internally. Your employees are also your customers. The success of your word-of-mouth marketing program depends partially on the quality of the customer service you provide to your employees. The old adage is true— your employees will treat customers the way you treat your employees.

Working with Your Customers

Your next step in controlling the word-of-mouth marketing program is to work with your customers. Be visible to your customers and talk with them on a regular basis. Get their opinions and suggestions on how you can make things better for them. Ask why they do business with you. Find out why they purchase from you instead of a competitor. Ask why they stay with you instead of changing stores or consultants. Once you have asked these questions, listen very carefully to their answers. The answers will guide your business.

If you listen to them, your customers will provide you with more information about your own business and your competitors' businesses than you ever dreamed possible. You will be able to structure your entire marketing program to take advantage of the many opportunities your customers present to you. The more you listen to them, the more they will want to go out and market for you (e.g., increase referrals). When you implement their suggestions internally, your external "sales" force multiplies exponentially.

Help your customers market for you. Educate them and give them simple and effective things to tell their friends. Remember that the successful journey begins with one small step. Reward them for their small, yet successful steps. After they have become a referral source for you, cultivate them and give them even more information to tell their friends. The more you get them involved in your business, the more involved they will want to become and remain.

Referrals and positive word-of-mouth will not come just because you do a good job or happen to be a nice person. Remember, you need to educate and train your customers to provide referrals for you. You must train them in the types of referrals you want, teach them what to say to people, ask them for referrals and help them make the referrals to you.

As customers make referrals to your business, thank them with a reward program. Think of how you want to recognize and reward the positive word-of-mouth that your customers generate for you.

Other Ways to Create Positive Word-of-Mouth

Here are several other ways for you to generate positive word-of-mouth.

Be novel. Be outrageous or outlandish. Be unique. Be different. Do something different. Host an extra-special event. And always make sure whatever you do is positive and has a good and beneficial outcome for everyone.

People love novelty and uniqueness. In fact, there was something unique about you that first made them become your customer. Now, do something else new and unique. Keep your business fresh and innovative. Ask people for new ideas and try them out. Be creative. Contact the media. If it is new, creative and innovative, they may want to cover it. Once they publicize it, you have tremendous third party, credible, word-of-mouth advertising about your business.

There it is. Your basic how-to on word-of-mouth marketing. Begin with your employees. Listen to, educate and train your customers, and recognize and reward everyone for their efforts on your behalf. Always try to be unique and different. When you have something newsworthy to report, keep the media informed of what is occurring in your business. Use well-planned, positive word-of-mouth to generate publicity for your business and be prepared to benefit from the publicity.

One Last Thought

Some people include a publicity-generating technique called seeding as part of their word-of-mouth marketing program. Seeding is when you, as someone other than yourself, or someone else calls up the media or any other influential person and requests information on your business. You are planting a seed in their minds about some feature or aspect of your business. When enough people do this, the media person begins to think there may be a story behind this business. They may call you and do that story, which does generate the publicity you were seeking.

The seeding strategy may appear to be successful, and it sometimes works. However, be aware of two things when you use seeding.

First, if the media find out there is really no story there, their negative word-of-mouth can bury your business. You cannot fight the media, especially if they retaliate because you used them by seeding stories to them. They will not care nor will they want to know that you were just trying to generate publicity by using this approach. While they may not publish anything negative, they may never publish anything positive again.

Second, what will happen to you or your business if this influential person whom you have cultivated and now seeded a story to finds out you were seeding a story, and there really is nothing to the story? They will feel used. How will you turn around their thoughts, feelings and negative word-of-mouth? How will you handle the negative publicity, either explicit or implicit, that their influence can generate? How will you respond to your customers who get a bad taste in their mouths over what you have done?

In contrast, at times seeding has been used effectively. Companies of all sizes in all industries seed their publicity stories to generate the word-of-mouth they desire. Not every company does it, nor is seeding good or bad. I am presenting it to you as another technique for your word-of-mouth marketing program. You decide if, when and how you will use it.

Word-of-mouth marketing is not a substitute for a good marketing plan and an overall marketing program. Word-of-mouth is just one component of a comprehensive marketing plan. Like other aspects of that plan, it must be controlled, used and measured to determine if it achieves its desired benefits.

Never leave your word-of-mouth marketing to chance. Use the strategies and techniques described here and make word-of-mouth work for you. It will become an integral and positive addition to your marketing program.

ASK YOURSELF

► Discuss what are you doing now that is so important, so newsworthy, that you must write a press release and backgrounder on it to inform everyone.

► Identify the most important people for you to contact at your local newspapers, radio and television stations.

• Describe what must you do to schedule a personal appointment with each of these media contacts?

• How will you prevent your presentation from appearing self-serving?

► Discuss how you will control your word-of-mouth marketing.

► What do your employees say about your products and services?

► What do your customers say about your products and services?

► What do your competitors say about your products and services?

► Describe the changes you will make, based upon what your employees, customers and competitors say about your products and services.

CHAPTER
SIX

DIRECT
MARKETING

HOW TO GET CUS- TOMERS TO CALL, WRITE AND COME IN TO BUY

A retailer who did not understand why her marketing program and advertising campaigns were not working contacted me recently for assistance. Her clothing store was spending more than $1,500 a week in newspaper ads, fliers and mailers. The results were not even generating enough revenue to cover the cost of the ads. When she called, this had been going on for three months. Since this is a great deal of money for a small business to be spending without receiving an appropriate return, I understood her concern. I reviewed her materials and found the following.

The newspaper ads were the typical copycat, everyday variety that clothing stores place in papers. The ads told people what the store was selling and at what price. The telephone number and address of the store were in small print at the bottom of the ad. Her fliers were basic, one-page descriptions of specials, with the store name and phone number on them. There was nothing fancy or eye catching, and no coupon or call to action. Finally, the direct mail pieces were part of a larger group marketing packet, with nothing to distinguish her coupon from the rest. Follow closely the suggestions I gave her, so you will not have to pay for the same costly mistakes.

THE BASICS OF DIRECT RESPONSE MARKETING

All marketing must be direct marketing. Institutional ads, designed to provide the reader with information and maintain a corporate image, are not effective. Although some businesses think these types of ads are revenue generators, they are a waste of money for most small businesses.

Any small business that engages in image advertising or places institutional ads—also known as tombstone ads, and you can guess why by now—is wasting money. No small business, regardless of size and annual revenues, can afford to use image advertising instead of direct response. All marketing must have a call to action. Something in your communication must motivate the reader to act now, to call, write or come in and become a customer.

Look at your newspaper ads. See if they have a call to action in them. If not, you can simply add "call now" with your telephone number in bigger, bolder letters than the rest of the ad. Bolding and capitalizing the letters and numbers is more effective than only giving the phone number. It makes the call to action stand out. Improve your call now command with termination dates for the offer, such as "expires at the end of this month," or "this offer is good only to the first 100 people who call or come in." Do something to generate a response. Your goal is to increase the sense of urgency and time pressure for the reader to respond, and to motivate them to do something to get in touch with you.

What motivates you to action? What motivates people you know to buy something? Ask your employees what motivated them to work for you. Ask your customers why they buy from you. Ask people in the street, or in your competitors' stores, what motivates them to buy and shop where they do. Also ask all these people what discourages them. Collect as much practical information as possible and use it as your call to action.

If you sell to different groups, such as young and old, or male and female, be aware that they will have different motivators. Your ads should reflect these in the call to action, based on the particular group you are marketing to. People like to be given direction and told what and how to do something. When you place a newspaper ad or use radio or television that gives information and does not tell the reader to call you or come see you, you are wasting money. If you do not tell the reader to come in to tour your store or to buy now before the prices increase, you are wasting money on your ad and marketing program.

Basic motivators include greed, fear, security, success, recognition, problem solutions and ways to save time, money and effort. Do your ads or marketing communications address these basic motivators? If not, what do you have to do to focus on these calls to action?

Now, back to the clothing store. How did I improve the store's ad? I changed two things. I created a benefit statement headline to replace the informational title, and, I targeted the headline and the ad copy to 30- to 45-year-olds. We know from research that this age group does not want to grow old, gracefully or otherwise. They will fight it every inch of the way. I used this need when I created the benefit headline "If You Are Growing Toward Middle Age, You Do Not Have To Grow In The Middle." We showed a before picture of real people in this age group, with slightly bulging middles, struggling as they tried to fit into tight jeans. The after picture showed these same people smiling and happy, wearing jeans that were a little looser around the middle. This was intended to get their interest because they could relate to the pictures and the problems. They would be motivated to come into the store to buy, since we would provide them with clothes that appear to fit well and make the people appear to be youthful enough to wear them. You may recall a television commercial for a national jean company that used a concept similar to this one.

The ad copy supported the headline and discussed the benefits of feeling comfortable while looking youthful. The call to action was to come in for a free fashion consultation session, related to youthful aging. The idea was to get people into the store and use the staff, store and displays to sell them on purchases.

She ran the ad once and got 14 calls for fashion consultations. She had to stop running the ad because her staff could not handle the consultations and their floor responsibilities. Currently, the store is again struggling. They have reduced their advertising expenses because of their reduced revenues. They are not marketing strategically for their small business.

This example demonstrates how to make your marketing and advertising direct response, and how to use direct response marketing effectively. Here are five reasons why you should use direct response marketing in your overall marketing campaign. Direct response marketing is:

1. *Targeted*—You know exactly which groups you are marketing to.

2. *Measurable*—You can track the effectiveness of your marketing efforts. This creates accountability and "contributability" to your marketing success.

Measurement, tracking and evaluation of direct marketing efforts are critical to the success of your future efforts.

3. *Personal*—You know about the people receiving your marketing message or mailer.

4. *Testable*—You can test every aspect of your direct response campaign, especially if you are using direct mail. This includes headlines, copy, offers, calls to action, prices and formats.

5. *Flexible*—You can change any aspect of your direct marketing campaign to suit your needs or the requirements of your customer group. This is especially true with direct mail.

Use Coupons to Increase Responses

You may have what appears to be the greatest headline and offer in the world. It will help to do one other thing to increase the response to your marketing campaign or communication: Include a coupon.

Coupons are easy to develop and can be attached to almost anything: ads, fliers, brochures and stand-alone pieces. A coupon can be sent in for more information, to receive a discount on something or placed in a prize pool. Lead boxes, which many commercial fitness centers, photography studios and travel agencies use, are nothing more than information-requesting or prize-entering coupons.

The ads in the store example could have had a coupon attached to them, asking people to mail or bring in the coupon for something or to receive information on how to shop wisely. The primary benefit of receiving coupons in the mail or in person from a prospective customer is that the store can develop a mailing list of interested—qualified—buyers. You can contact these people again and invite them into the store for a tour, a free fashion show or anything else, and then sell them clothing or whatever product you are selling.

When small businesses send out mailers to try to elicit a response from customers, they often do two things wrong. The mailer is often just an information piece. It says "Hi, I'm here doing such-and-such business, and I would like you to come into my store." Sometimes, there is a coupon or flier in the mailer, but the copy is not strong enough to motivate the reader to action. The second mistake is sending someone just a brochure about your business. Brochures alone are never enough. A letter always gets a better response than an information piece, whether a flier or brochure, that is sent alone. A letter and a brochure/flier leads to an even greater response. Add a coupon and your responses increase dramatically. Therefore, if you are sending out a mail piece to prospective buyers, make sure you back up your cover letter with fliers, brochures, coupons or all three. This will improve the results of your direct mail and marketing campaign.

Summary of Direct Marketing Basics

Make sure all your marketing communications, messages and advertising, are direct response-oriented. Always use hidden commands such as call now, call this number, write, come in, or anything else that moves and motivates the person reading or hearing your message to do something. Use coupons that require people to mail them back or to come in to redeem them for something. This involves customers in your marketing and helps you create a mailing list of interested buyers.

When you use direct mail, always use an updated list of customers and prospects. Include a letter with your material. The key to success in direct mail starts with a good and current list. You need to have your mail delivered to the right person, and a good list increases your chances of reaching the correct, prospective clients. Once you get the recipient to open the mail, they must read it. Letters are more personal and they tend to be read before they are thrown away. Letters are definitely read more often than information pieces. So, use a letter.

After you contact your prospects and have their attention, be prepared to respond effectively to your direct marketing efforts. Make certain there are enough materials to respond to requests for information and enough staff members to assist potential buyers and clients when they come into the store or office. Make yourself available to meet as many of these prospects as possible. When the owner or president pays personal attention to a prospect, that person feels much more important and is more likely to buy his or her goods and services.

Your Turn

▶ List all the direct marketing strategies, tactics and techniques you can think of. Place a star next to the ones you use in your business.

▶ If you are using direct mail, review your materials. Look for benefit statements, headlines that scream benefits, and irresistible offers. When you find your best ones, write them below. If you cannot find good ones or you do not use direct mail now, create some headlines and benefit statements, write them below and try to make them even better.

▶ Go to the library and look up books on direct marketing and direct mail. Copy any material that interests you or that you think can help you in your business. Modify that material to suit your specific direct marketing needs. It is not necessary to reinvent the wheel.

TESTING YOUR OFFERS

Testing is one of the most important aspects of direct response marketing and direct mail. I have separated it from the basic principles to emphasize its importance and to help you recognize that testing permeates every aspect of direct mail/marketing. You test your target market, your list, your offers, your ads, your copy, your mail pieces, your call to action, your fulfillment system and your tracking mechanisms.

Let us say you have been successful with your first direct mail or marketing campaign; you want to conduct another one. Here is a great opportunity to test some aspects of the campaign against new ideas to determine which campaign is more effective and productive.

Go back to your first mailing, if that is what you are using. Assume your target market was in one zip code and possessed certain characteristics that you specified. You now want to mail to two zip codes on opposite sides of your city. You select lists of names that match the same criteria as your first mailing; now you can test different aspects of the new mailing. You can send one offer, headline or price to one group and a different set of information to the other. Or you can keep everything the same and vary just one aspect of the mailing, such as the price or the headline. I recommend the latter approach to testing direct mail pieces: Vary only one aspect of the mailing at a time. Change the headline, the price, the response mechanism or the offer. If you vary more than one item, you have no way of knowing what caused the response. Keep tests of your mailings simple, trackable and controllable. Mail the entire test at the same time.

Constantly test your direct marketing strategies and direct mail pieces. Do not get complacent because a mailing or technique pulls a satisfactory response. How do you know that by changing just one aspect of the mailing you would not increase your response rate by 10%? There are instances of higher prices outpulling lower prices because of the perception of the target audience relative to the product being sold. There are also instances of no free offers doing better than mailings with free offers. Unless you test your mail pieces against each other, you will never know this.

Test one mailing against another to see which delivers the best response, based on whatever response criteria you establish. This can be number of inquiries, store visits, dollar purchases, units purchased or telephone inquiries. You determine the criteria for tracking your mailer or direct response effort. When you have a clear winner, which should be 15% better than your current control, use the winner as your control and develop another direct mail piece to compete with it. Again, vary one item at a time in this second piece, such as the headline, the price of your product or service or your offer. Determine which piece pulls better. Select that as your control. Use the 15% differential as your criteria for success. After four or five tests, if you have one piece that continues to outperform the others, use it until the responses and inquiries start to dry up.

One other point about direct marketing and direct mail campaigns also holds true for advertisements. Once you have found a campaign that proves to be successful, use it again and again. Because you are used to seeing the material, you will get tired of it long before your customers and prospects do. Your list will tell you when they are tired of your campaign by not buying from you anymore. Until that happens, keep using ads or direct mail offers that work.

Direct mail is probably the most well known of direct response marketing. It is important to know about it and how to use it (see Chapter 7), as well as the other direct marketing methods that can make your small business more successful. All of them must make some type of offer to your potential customer and call them to action. Here are some basic ways to make your offers motivating. Adapt them for your own use.

DIRECT MARKETING OFFERS

The headline of your direct marketing piece, letter, brochure or flier is what gains the reader's or listener's attention. However, sometimes even a weak headline can be saved by a great offer. Here are ways to make your offers great and improve the quality of your direct marketing campaigns.

Basically you can make three types of offers. They should all appeal to satisfying some basic need, such as security, greed, fear, receiving a reward or respect for authority. The three offers are discounts or free trials, special assistance and guarantees. Some businesses even make all three offers in a single marketing communication. As long as you can fulfill your promises, there is nothing wrong with that approach.

Discounts can be offered to customers who pay cash, who pay by a certain date, who buy several products or services at one time, or who purchase multiples of one item. Discounts can be extended to their ultimate level by offering something for free, such as a free trial program, a free book or a free gift with a purchase of some type or expense.

Special assistance offers provide people with the knowledge that they will receive help. You may offer financing for purchases, accept credit cards, provide totally supervised tours, accept trade-ins on products, accept exchanges from competitors, extend credit for specific reasons, or even provide valet parking or taxi service. Several hospitals provide van and taxi services for their patients at no extra charge. When a patient has a choice of hospitals, which do you think stands out in their mind?

Guarantees are very powerful offers. The most powerful of these is the unconditional, money-back guarantee if the customer is not completely satisfied. This type of guarantee is also known as risk reversal, where you are assuming all the risk. Magazine and book publishers use this a great deal. They send you a publication that you can keep for fifteen or thirty days, to decide if you like it. If not, you can send it back to them. They assume all the risk by allowing you to "own" the publication and try their product for a specified period of time without paying for it.

Adapt this approach to your business. Allow people to participate in your programs for free, for a specified period of time. State this boldly in your direct mail offer. The word free is a powerful motivator. For example, if you conduct seminars, offer the participants their money back if they are not completely satisfied. An even greater guarantee and risk reversal is to tell them in your direct mail piece that they must call or write in to register, but do not have to pay until the end, or middle, of the program. If, at the time payment is required, they do not believe they are getting their money's worth, they can leave and not pay.

I know of a speaker who has seminar participants send in their registration fee up-front, but does not cash the checks. The uncashed checks are available at the registration table for any participant who wants to leave by lunch on the first day of the program. The risk is entirely reversed from the participant to the speaker. The check sent up front is merely a formality, for registration purposes. Imagine the effect the participant has when reading the direct mail solicitation or ad that says you can pick up your uncashed check at the registration table by lunch, if you are not completely satisfied or if you do not believe the program is worth more than you paid for it.

Another type of guarantee is the guaranteed, discount/renewal rate. Health clubs and newsletter publishers use this a great deal in their direct marketing. You can adapt it for your business. A guaranteed discount renewal rate tells readers that if they make a purchase now and send payment or have already made a purchase, they can guarantee future purchases—club memberships or subscription renewals—at a lower rate. Some businesses even offer a gift for prompt payment.

Check your magazine or newsletter subscriptions. See how many times they send you early renewal notices, telling you about the great discount you will receive if you pay now. Ask yourself how many times have you responded to these offers. Although this may seem like a hard-core sales closing technique, if it is worded properly in your direct mail piece, it can increase your response levels. Why do direct marketers use it? It works.

If you are having trouble developing an offer or call to action for any of your direct marketing programs, go back and review what you are offering. Re-evaluate your products or services. Brainstorm with others about the best offer to make and the best way to make it. Remember that the best offer is the one that motivates your target market to act.

STILL MORE DIRECT MARKETING METHODS

Newsletters

You should consider several other direct marketing methods. The newsletter is the one that is most familiar to people. It is a great way to keep prospects and customers, and even competitors, informed about your business. Here are seven tips to help you publish a successful newsletter—one that generates customers who buy from you:

1. *Write it as an information piece.* Provide your readers with information about your business, news about the readers themselves and talk about your employees. Do not sell in your newsletter. The fact that you are providing information informs people that you are an expert. They will know to come to you if they need what you provide.

2. *Make it easy to read.* Use type sizes large enough for your audience to read easily. Keep the sentences and the paragraphs short, use graphics and illustrations to complement the text and use two to three columns. People are used to reading newspapers in columns; this skill will transfer to your newsletter. Do not re-invent the wheel. Use what you know works in other areas.

3. *Publish on time.* Make certain you stick to whatever schedule you develop for the newsletter. Your readers will be expecting it, especially if they like what you have to say.

4. *Quality vs quantity.* It is not necessary to publish a four- or eight-page newsletter for it to be effective. I work with someone who sends out a quarterly, one-page, two-column newsletter as a self-mailer to all his clients. It is extremely effective because of the information in it.

   I also work with someone who publishes an excellent newsletter on marketing for small businesses. I recommend it because the information in the newsletter is accurate and valuable to small business owners. You can receive a free trial issue of *The Antin Marketing Letter— Secrets From The Lost Art of Common Sense Marketing,* by calling 813-468-2000. This eight-page monthly newsletter is written in the letter of news format.

   In any newsletter, regardless of format, say what you have to say in as small a space as possible. Make the information valuable and interesting. They will appreciate your quality; do not fill up pages just to produce quantity.

5. *Make a free offer.* Since I already told you not to sell anything within the newsletter, make a free offer. This will not be perceived as selling and will be appreciated by your readers. Offer them a free gift if they come in and make a purchase. Offer them a free trial of something. Or offer to send a free copy of your newsletter to someone they recommend.

6. *Use inserts.* If your newsletter is four or more pages, use inserts. These are free-standing pages that tell another story. This story can be completely different from the content of the newsletter. The insert does not have to be a story at all. It can be a blatant advertisement to sell something.

This is not contradictory to what I said originally about not selling in the newsletter. You are not selling in the newsletter. You are selling in the insert. The insert is perceived as a completely separate piece from the newsletter. Readers will welcome the opportunity to purchase something from the insert, especially if the offer is discounted. Make sure the insert has a direct response mechanism, such as a coupon or telephone number. By selling through inserts, the integrity of the newsletter is preserved.

7. *Give it away.* This may sound like silly advice, but if you are using the newsletter to promote your business, services or products, you should give it away. You should even pay for the postage. Now, if you are trying to start a subscription newsletter, whose information content is more general, that is another story. But, if it is just a prospect/customer/client newsletter, make sure you foot the bill and give it away. The response you get to it will more than make up for the minimal investment in paper and postage.

These seven tips will help make your newsletter much more successful. Now, here is an interesting twist on the newsletter idea.

Letter of News

As a small business owner, you should be sending correspondence to your customers and visitors—prospects—on a regular basis. You can add another piece of correspondence that I call a letter of news. This is essentially a newsletter, written in a letter format. You use similar subheadings and content material as in newsletters, and you can cover different or more personalized topics.

People get a variety of newsletters to read; many of those are never read, are only skimmed or get thrown away before they are read. No one can read everything. You need to break through this information clutter and get your material read by your customers and prospects. Your personalized letter of news will do this for you. It will definitely get read because its appearance is the same as a personal letter, and everyone loves to get personal mail.

Keep the tone of your letter very friendly, while still providing the important information your readers need to know. If possible, use your computer to personalize the address. You will find that you can make offers, sell items and even ask people for referrals in the letter of news without harming the integrity of the piece. This is somewhat different than selling directly through a traditional newsletter. However, if you are concerned about causing a negative reaction to a sales presentation in your letter of news, attach an insert—a separate flier or brochure—to the letter, and let the stand-alone piece sell for you.

Brochures and Fliers

Brochures and fliers are two other direct marketing pieces you can use. They can be included in a direct mail campaign, they can be given out directly to people at meetings and functions or they can be left on cars in parking lots—with permission. Brochures and fliers provide potential customers with important information about your business in a capsulized form. They may be brief, but they should be powerful and motivating.

Brochures and fliers must be eye-appealing. Make certain they promote the benefits of whatever you are selling. Forget the features. People are only interested in benefits; since you do not have much space on these pieces, you must identify the benefits you want to sell and then sell them to the hilt.

To save money, many business owners write and design their own brochures and then take them to a quick printer. Although they do save money, my experience is that these brochures are not nearly as well done as they can be. People find it inherently difficult to brag about themselves and their business. They tend to write in a more technical, informational mode than a selling mode. The art and graphics are seldom what they should be. Therefore, owners rarely develop a brochure that is as good as one developed by an outside, objective professional.

Regardless of your budget, seek professional assistance if you want a quality brochure. Graphic artists, marketing consultants, copywriters and others who have experience in preparing brochures can help you produce a successful brochure. Your brochure and flier become the customer or prospect's image of your business. Since they must sell for you when you are not there, make sure they represent the image you want to portray.

You may also be able to get this professional assistance for free. Offer to trade out something with the experts who will help you produce the brochure or flyer. Barter is an excellent marketing technique and one that you should strongly consider using as often as possible.

Direct Marketing Creativity

Creativity is essential to success in marketing, especially direct marketing. Do not think, even for a minute, that your direct marketing efforts and direct mail pieces have to be of a standard, everyday, routine variety. Just because your competitors send out copycat pieces or run look-alike ads, does not mean you have to do the same.

The more creative you are with your direct marketing, the better your chances for success. Some creative ideas include different types of envelopes or packaging for your pieces, more stamps on the envelope, using calligraphy to address the envelopes, using window or double-window envelopes, sending a mailgram first or sending a telegram to watch for the mail. You may want to try some of these concepts.

If you own a lumber yard, why not mail a small piece of wood to prospects? Imprint a message on the wood about your business and make them an offer. You will be pleasantly surprised at the response.

If you own a yogurt store, mail people who live and work within a mile of your store a plastic cone. Imprint the cone with your name, address and telephone number and an invitation to come in and trade the plastic cone for a real cone, free. Again, your responses will surprise you.

Your Turn

What other creative direct marketing ideas can you come up with? Do not limit yourself to traditional thinking. Open up your mind, allow yourself to be outrageous, and you will be surprised at the results.

Telemarketing

Telemarketing is another excellent direct marketing technique. Telemarketing is contacting people on the phone, explaining to them who you are and the purpose of your call, learning about their needs and requirements, and making them the same offer you would make in print or in person. The key to success in telemarketing is the same as it is in other types of marketing: You select the target market, identify their needs and make them an offer they find irresistible, which will satisfy those needs.

People often raise a question about a telemarketing script—should one be developed and used, or should telemarketers just improvise? The following suggestion has proven to be successful in telemarketing campaigns in a variety of industries.

There are two types of telemarketing scripts: formal and informal. A formal script details everything the telemarketer must say on each call and describes typical responses the prospect will make based on what the telemarketer says. The telemarketer often has a flow chart to identify where to go next in the script when the person called responds in a certain way. There can be no deviation by anyone from a formal telemarketing script.

Formal scripts should definitely be used for telemarketers who are new to your business, regardless of their experience, and for inexperienced telemarketers. If the scripts have been successful in the past in attracting new customers to your store or business, they should not be changed. Only revise or write a new formal script when the current one stops working.

As you would do for an ad or a direct mail campaign, use it as long as it works. Remember, you will probably get tired of the script before your customers do. Even if you are tired of it, use it as long as it keeps people buying from you.

An informal telemarketing script is basically an outline of what should be said on the phone. Informal scripts should only be used by experienced and successful telemarketers who know your business. They must be capable of carrying on the sales conversation with the prospect as if it was spontaneous. Informal scripts allow telemarketers to inject their own personality and experiences into the call, which makes the call more personal.

Never allow telemarketers to say whatever they want to say, rather than what they are supposed to say. All telemarketers should be giving out the same information and making the same offers. As the business owner, you must determine if there is any leeway in this procedure. You can give your telemarketers the authority to make adjustments or offer additional discounts within certain ranges if that is what it takes to make the sale, but you must make certain the offers from all your telemarketers are basically the same. If this needs to be done through a formal script with no deviation, do it this way. It is better for your marketing efforts to have every-one saying and doing the same thing than to have employees giving out different, or possibly, wrong information.

The same concept holds true for people answering incoming calls. They are also telemarketers. They must be prepared to answer the phone properly and respond to any questions or situations that may arise.

An effective way to answer the telephone at your store or office is to always answer by the third or fourth ring. Then, have the person say "Good morning (afternoon, evening), 'name of your business.' This is (employee's name). How may I help you?"

Answering in this way motivates the caller to provide you with more information about their call. If you answer "Can I help you?" the caller can just say no. It is like the salesperson who approaches a customer in a store and asks "Can I help you?"; the customer usually answers, "No, I'm just looking." If the question is "How may I help you?" the customer has to answer with more than just yes or no.

When you speak with people either on the phone or in person, always try to use statements, phrases or questions that elicit information from them. This way, you reduce the possibility of a miscommunication and prevent them from ending the conversation abruptly with a yes or no answer.

People hate to be placed on hold, especially if you have called them to sell them something. Avoid placing a prospect or customer on hold when you make outgoing telemarketing calls. If you must place the caller on hold, either on an incoming or outgoing call, explain why they are being placed on hold and ask them if they mind. Never answer a phone by saying "Please hold," and putting them on hold before they can respond or tell you why they called. What if they want to buy thousands of dollars worth of products from you, but hang up instead because they did not like being put abruptly on hold?

If you have to transfer the caller to someone else, tell the caller what you are doing and why, and that it will be your pleasure to transfer them so they can get the help they need.

A Simple and Effective Telemarketing Script

Many businesspeople shy away from telemarketing because they either do not like the impersonal rejection that occurs on the telephone or they have difficulty getting to speak to the decision maker. Below is a brief script that will help you get through to the decision maker if you are doing business-to-business telemarketing. A second script will help you overcome the decision maker's reluctance to listen to your telephone sales presentation:

Getting through the Gatekeeper (Secretary/Receptionist)

YOU: I'd like to speak with Mr. Prospect, please.

SEC: Who is calling?

YOU: This is [your name] with [your business or company name]. Who am I speaking with?

SEC: This is Joan. May I ask the nature of your call?

YOU: Joan, I am calling Mr. Prospect with the information he was looking for on . . . (insert your business here).

SEC: Was he expecting your call?

YOU: No, Joan, not at this exact time, but he was waiting to hear from me. Could you please tell him that I am on the line? Thank you.

SEC: One moment please. I'll see if he's in.

This should get you through to the decision maker. If he is not available and you have to call back, try to schedule a time to call back when he will be there to take your call. Once you reach him, here is what you can say:

YOU: Mr. Prospect?

HIM: Yes, this is Mr. Prospect.

YOU: Mr. Prospect, this is [your name] with [your business or company name]. I am calling with your information on . . . This information will help you [your company] . . . [insert two or three benefits here for him]. Is there any reason you would not be interested in hearing more about these benefits?

HIM: No, go right ahead.

At this point you can begin your presentation.

These scripts have worked as they are, and with slight variations, for consultants, insurance agents, stock brokers, sales reps and other business-to-business marketers. You can also adapt the scripts for use with customers whom you call at home.

These few hints on telemarketing, using scripts and answering the telephone will help you be more successful in your direct marketing efforts.

One Last Thought on Direct Marketing

Typical responses to direct marketing are about 1% or 2%. You can create increased responses simply by following up your direct marketing piece with a personal telephone call. In fact, if you use a technique called response compression, you will possibly increase your response rate to more than 5% or 10%.

Response compression involves multiple contacts with a customer or prospect within a short period of time—no more than two weeks. For example, you would mail a piece to a prospect on a Monday, call on Friday to make certain he or she received the piece, mail another piece on Monday, call again on Wednesday, and call again on Friday. The objective of all these contacts is to schedule an appointment with the prospect, to get him or her to visit your store or to buy something from you, and to begin to develop a relationship with this person. Remember that the more familiar you are to a prospect, the greater the chances of their doing business with you.

How to Improve Your Direct Response Marketing Campaigns

Below is a brief summary of several ways to improve your direct response marketing.

► *Sales Letters*

- Personalize the letter

- Use and personalize a response device or reply card

- Target the letter individually to each of your target audiences

- Encourage both telephone and mail responses

- Use short sentences and short paragraphs with sub-headings

- Offer something tangible for the reader to send for: a brochure, flier, bribe, bonus gift or other incentive

- Offer something extra for readers to receive if they buy now

- Mail first class or overnight

- Sign the letter in blue ink so the reader knows it is an original

- End a page in the middle of a sentence so the reader must continue on to the next page

- Use a headline if you have a good one

► *Envelopes*

- Use a different color or different size envelope

- Write provocative and motivating teaser copy on the envelope

- Use stamps or a meter instead of an indicia

- Make up the proper postage with multiple stamps

- Use unique envelopes, such as ones with double windows

- Use a handwritten envelope to make it look more personal

- Write free on the envelope if you are giving something away

- Keep all inserts to a size that does not bulge the envelope

▶ *Print Ads*

- Make the headline benefits-oriented
- Keep the headline straightforward and not cute or clever
- Use humor only if you are 100% certain the reader will understand it
- Make the ad direct response—use a coupon or phone number
- Create a code to track responses to the ad
- Run the ad on a right-hand page in the publication
- Stress and restress the free offer in your copy
- Put the free offer in your headline
- Use pictures
- If you have one, include your 800 number
- Keep the copy interesting

▶ *Brochures*

- Make it a sales piece
- Include check boxes or questions to involve the reader
- Include a questionnaire or specification sheet to help qualify the prospect
- Lead the reader to a specific course of action
- Write the copy so it answers more and more questions as the reader goes through the brochure
- Make it easy to find and read your address and phone number
- If you are using a reply card as part of the brochure, make it easy to tear off—show where it should be cut or torn off

▶ *Press Releases*

- Make sure the headline has strong reader interest

- Tell the reader the information mentioned in the release is available in more detail from you

- Mention your free booklet or offer in the headline

- Make certain your release is topical

- If the release is two or more pages, make sure each page ends in the middle of a sentence

- Lead the reader to a course of action

- Make your name, address and phone number easy to find on the release and even in the body of the release

- Send a sample of your free offer to the editor

▶ *Articles*

- Try to get published in the most popular or widely read publications in your field; if you cannot, any publication is better than none at all

- Have the editor include your biography at the end of your article, which includes your name, company number, address, telephone numbers and information about your product or service

- Publishing the article is more important than getting paid for writing it (If you cannot get paid, try to trade for free ad space)

- Run an ad with your article on the same page (If this position is not available, run it on the page facing your article or as close to the article as possible)

- If you are giving something away, mention it in the article and leave it up to the editor whether to include it or cut it out

- Make your title benefits-oriented
- Use bullet points, lists and short paragraphs to increase readership
- Reprint the articles as publicity pieces, free reports, and tip sheets (e.g., *Ten Tips on Low-Cost, No-Cost Marketing Techniques*)
- Show your expertise in the article and invite readers to contact you

▶ *Presentations, Seminars, Speeches and Workshops*

- Be informative, not promotional—the fact that you are giving the program will be promotional enough
- If you must promote yourself or your business during the program, let the audience know you will do this and when it will occur
- Educate, educate, educate during the program
- Provide handouts with your name, company name, address and telephone number on them so people can contact you after the program
- Offer free booklets, in addition to the handout material
- Make sure everyone registers before sitting down (capture their name, address, telephone number and, if possible, how they heard of the program)
- Write your own introduction and have someone else read it to the attendees; list your credentials and qualifications to impress the audience
- Tape your seminar or presentation and send it to attendees for free afterwards or sell it to them
- Make sure all attendees fill out an evaluation form and indicate on this form where they should write their name, address and phone number

- Write a thank you note to your host, if you did not self-promote the program

- If the audience was under 20 people, write each one a personal thank you note for attending.

These suggestions to improve your direct response marketing campaigns are taken from more than 15 years of experience as a marketing consultant and research into many other sources. In his book, *Business To Business Direct Marketing* (NTC Publishing, 4255 W. Touhy Ave., Lincolnwood, IL, 60646), Bob Bly expands on these ideas and recommends other catalogs, trade shows, columns, newsletters or company magazines, postcards and inquiry fulfillment materials.

ASK YOURSELF

► Review all your marketing and advertising material. What can you do to improve your calls to action? How can you make them more direct response-oriented?

► Are you using the telephone as a marketing tool? How effective are your efforts? What percentage of your sales is due to telephone contacts with customers?

► What is the best way for you to turn all your marketing and advertising campaigns into direct response marketing programs? (*Hint:* Talk to a friend about what you do and what you sell. Record this session. Get excited and tell this friend why people should buy from you. You will be focusing on benefits that customers will be interested in. Transcribe the recording and look for headlines and other benefit statements in your comments. You will also find calls to action.) Now, what would you do?

CHAPTER
SEVEN

DIRECT MAIL
MAGIC

HOW TO PULL CUSTOMERS OUT OF A HAT

A little knowledge about direct mail can definitely be dangerous. Eavesdrop with me on a conversation between two small business owners who are considering adding direct mail to their marketing mix. They have read books and articles on the topic and they are now discussing how they could use direct mail for their businesses.

The first owner tells the second that she read that direct mail is the most expensive form of marketing, since it is uncertain whether it will work well enough to provide an appropriate return on investment. The second owner agrees and says he heard that a good response to a direct mail campaign is 1%–2%. The conversation continues with both small business owners reciting statistics about direct mail to each other.

See what I mean by a little knowledge being dangerous? As long as they continue reciting statistics, they will talk themselves out of using what may be the most effective marketing technique.

It is true that these statistics are often quoted as facts in the direct mail industry, but you do not have to live by those statistics or be afraid of them. Follow the guidelines outlined below to increase your response rates and your revenue per response and lower your cost per response from your direct mail marketing campaign.

Before You Begin

Make certain that a direct mail program fits in well with the rest of your marketing plan. If you are using a direct mail campaign because your competitors are doing it or it seems like a good idea because of something you read or a seminar you attended, stop. You will be wasting your money and time.

Your direct mail programs must be developed as an integral part of your overall marketing plan. When the time is right, begin your direct mail campaign.

Test the Waters

Start with a small test area such as a five-mile radius around your store, office or, for home-based businesses, home, or specific companies in a particular industry or within a certain geographical location. Keep the initial mailing small, no more than a few hundred pieces or one coupon pack if you are involved in a group mailing such as *Val-Pack, Advo* or *Stuff-it.* This allows you to test the mailing itself, track the results, and respond properly to the inquiries or orders. If the materials and offer work, expand your mailing area.

If you use a mailing list, start with a small portion of that list; if the initial mailing is successful, go to a larger portion. Never, never try a first-time direct mail campaign with a large market area or large list.

One other point you must be aware of. If your mailing succeeds or fails, it is due to one of these factors: the mailing list, the offer, the ad or letter, the price, or a combination of these. This is why you must start with a small test area, see if the mailing works, and then change one thing, such as the headline, letter or price, before you test another small area or part of the list. You can only develop a successful direct mail campaign by testing everything in your package against itself.

Your Turn

▶ Describe the differences between direct mail and direct response marketing.

▶ Identify your test market area. What are the specifications and characteristics of the people or businesses you want to reach?

▶ Who else do you know that uses direct mail in their business? Make an appointment with them to discuss how they do it and how it works for them. Find out how they would improve it.

PRINCIPLES OF SUCCESSFUL DIRECT MAIL

Principle #1: Scratch the Niche

The foundation of success in direct mail is the mailing list. Although the list is extremely important, it is more important to determine your target market. Who are the people you want to contact? What are their identifying characteristics? How old are they? What is their income? How and why do they buy certain goods and services? What ideas, values, beliefs, desires and needs do they have in common? Basically, you are determining what niche market they fit into.

Many small business owners and entrepreneurs opt for the small fish in the big pond approach. They figure there is enough to go around for everybody—they are wrong. Look around the business community where you live and work and read your newspapers. The big fish are gobbling up the little fish. If you think being a little fish in a big pond is good and healthy for you, I sure hope you can swim real fast from the sharks.

You need to be either a big fish in a little pond or build your own pond—create your own niche market for your business. Then you own the entire pond or market. These are the two best ways to access a niche market. If you are the big fish in the little pond—niche market—or you own the entire pond, it makes it very difficult for competitors to come in for a swim. The fewer competitors you have to face, the bigger your market share and greater your revenues. For marketing in general and direct mail in particular, select a niche market that you want to target, and tell them your story.

After identifying your target market, you are ready to select your mailing list.

Principle #2: The Name's the Thing

Your mailing list will make or break your direct mail campaign. Select the list carefully; it must be current and accurate. You can use two types of lists: internal and external.

An internal mailing list, also called a house list, comes from current and former customers of your business and visitors. If you are not tracking everyone who comes into your store or office and getting, at a minimum, their name, address and telephone number you should be—you are missing out on some tremendous money-making opportunities. Remember that these people have already shown an interest in what you are offering. They may need a little of your positive motivation to get them to buy. Keep this internal list up-to-date and ready for use.

Another way to generate an internal mailing list is to ask each of your employees and current customers to provide you with three names and addresses of people they think might be interested in receiving information about your business. You will be surprised how many names you will get for your list just by asking. People will help you succeed if you just ask and let them.

Your external mailing list will be much more defined than your internal one. Your internal list is based on characteristics of people who do business with you or whose names you have collected from one source or another. You are not paying directly for your internal list, so you use the information as it comes in. With an external mailing list, you can target your mailing. For example, specify their ages, gender, household income, residential or business zip code, number of family members, education level, purchasing habits and anything else you can think of that will more narrowly define your potential prospects.

When you have compiled all this information, contact a list broker to rent or purchase a list for you, rent or purchase the list for yourself from other list owners or look up names in the telephone book. This last method of getting an external list should only be used as a final resort, since you cannot identify characteristics of prospects from the telephone book.

Using a list broker is the safest way to ensure that your money will be well spent on a mailing list. List brokers are in business to match lists to your specifications, so you get the greatest return for your investment. If their lists do not pull for you, you will be dissatisfied, take your business elsewhere and/or give them a bad reference. Therefore, list brokers will do everything possible to help you select the best list available for your mailing.

You can help yourself when you use a list broker by asking the broker to provide you with references. You want to talk to other customers who have used these lists and learn the types of responses they received. You also want certain guarantees, such as that the list is current and has been updated within the last three to six months, and that they will reimburse you in some way for nondeliverables—those pieces that are returned to you or trashed. You want to receive a guarantee that the list is at least 90%–95% deliverable, or some other arrangements must be made, such as a reduction in price.

Purchasing a list from another list owner can have a major advantage and disadvantage. The advantage is you are fairly sure that the people on the list make purchases from mailings, or the list owner would not maintain and use that list. The disadvantage in using someone else's personal or house list is that there could be duplicate names, the list may not be current, and the list may not have been cleaned—purged of duplicates and incorrect addresses.

My first recommendation is that you buy a list from a reputable list broker. Use someone else's list if you cannot do this. As a last resort, create your own list from the telephone or other directories.

Here is a tip for small business owners who have compiled an accurate and current in-house list. Other businesses, both competitors and noncompetitors, will pay money to rent your list from you. Think about it—you have spent time and money developing your list. When you use it for direct mail, it works. Now you can charge others for the same privilege and start to recoup some of your list development costs.

Eventually, if you rent the list enough times, you will start making pure profit on each list rental. In effect, you become a list broker and the revenues from the list rentals becomes passive income.

You can find list brokers in your telephone book under mailing lists. Or, go to the library and read *Direct Mail List Rates and Data,* published by Standard Rate and Data Service.

Principle #3: Pay for Quality

Many small business owners begin their first venture into direct mail by looking for the least expensive list that comes closest to meeting their specifications. Worse than that, I have spoken with business owners who have rented a list, any list, because it looked like it might work. Why do people do these things? Because they want to spend as little as possible on this method of marketing. Cheap lists may work some of the time. More often than not, the response is poor. When you add the costs of the mailing to the poor response, the small business owner concludes that direct mail is not for his or her business. This is a mistake, because the quality of the list often determines the success of your mailing.

As with anything else, pay for quality.

You have developed your specifications for the mailing list, identified how you will secure the list and determined its deliverability and guarantees. Now you have to buy or rent the list. Lists usually cost anywhere from $10 to more than $100 per thousand names. Although cost is important, it is only important in the context of how many names on the list have purchased products or services similar to yours in the past, or how many of them have a predisposition to buy such items. The cost of a list does not always determine its quality, although more expensive lists usually contain names of the best mail order buyers and responders. Consider these quality lists when you decide on your campaign.

Some lists require that a premium be paid, depending on the number of names you want on a list. The list owner or broker may require you to purchase a minimum number of names. If this is your first mailing, purchase the minimum for your market area, test the list with your offer and, if the mailing is successful, buy more names to do a larger mailing.

One more point about lists. They can be purchased on magnetic tape for extraordinarily large mailings, on computer disks or on pressure labels. The price of the list may be affected by its format. Decide what and how you need the names before you buy any list.

Principle #4: Make Them an Offer They Cannot Refuse

It is time to create your direct mail piece or package. Regardless of what you are selling, this package must include an offer recipients cannot refuse. It must be so inviting, so irresistible and so motivating that the recipient has to call you, send you money to make a purchase or come see you now.

Be as creative and artistic as you want, but remember, the mailer is still a sales tool. As such, it must get the message across that the recipient will benefit more by purchasing from you now than by waiting or not purchasing at all.

The mail piece must be full of benefits. You are selling only benefits, not features of your products or services. People are only interested in what a product or service can do for them, how it can make them feel better or solve a problem they may have. If they can buy ways to realize their dreams, goals and hopes, they will buy from you. Your store or services are the vehicles for making that happen. Make sure your offer gives them exactly what they are hoping for and dreaming about.

Here are seven ways to improve your direct mail offer:

1. *The Envelope*—Do something different to the envelope. Write teaser or informational copy on it to get the recipient to open the envelope. Use words like "Urgent," "The information you requested," and "How would you like to . . .". Use odd-sized or colored envelopes. Send the mailer in what looks like a telegram envelope, an overnight envelope or a second-day air envelope. You

must do something to get people to open it. Otherwise, they will just throw your mailer in the garbage with the rest of the junk mail.

2. *Write from the Heart*—Your copy must be interesting, motivating and inviting. Write the way you speak. Use contractions, picture-provoking and sound-inducing words and phrases. Use cliches. And forget about that old argument that short copy is better than long copy. First, if your headline or opening is poor, no one will read your mailer anyway so the length of your copy does not matter. Second, people will read long copy as long as you keep it interesting. One more point: When you write long copy, keep the sentences and paragraphs short, indent, bold, italicize and capitalize for emphasis.

3. *Stamps*—Use first class postage or a postage meter. Do not use indicia. For an even better chance of getting envelopes opened, use multiple stamps that equal the correct postage. People are always interested in seeing what is inside an envelope could be so important that somebody took the time to put 12 five-cent stamps on a 60-cent mailing piece.

4. *Lift Letter*—The lift letter is a short note on a smaller piece of paper, written either by you or someone else, which works as an additional motivator to get the recipient to respond. You see lift letters all the time if you get sweepstakes mailers.

   Lift letters can be additional calls to action or third party endorsements. Use different colored paper or ink; make it handwritten, or print it in a different font. Just make it noticeable so the recipient will pick it up.

5. *Paper*—Change your paper stock. Be different and creative. Use nonstandard sizes and shapes. Use cards instead of letters. Remember, you must stand out.

6. *Color*—Color will always get a response in direct mail. Use colored paper, colored ink, or colored envelopes. Make certain your color selection fits the mood of your mailer. You probably do not want to use black if you are talking

about something happy. Similarly, if you are selling relaxation devices, too much red will work against you.

7. *Offer a Bribe*—This is an ethical bribe. Offer the recipient a free brochure, report, small gift, trial period of anything else you can think of to get them to try your product or service. If the word bribe bothers you, think of it as an incentive.

These seven ideas will give your offers a better chance of being opened and read. Once the prospect is looking at your mailer, it is up to you to have written captivating copy, along with an irresistible offer, to get them to do business with you. If you cannot do all these things by yourself, get a professional to help you.

Principle #5: Check Your Calendar

Never do a direct mail program indiscriminately. You should know from research in your industry what the peak buying months or buying cycles are. Schedule your mailing to coincide with those peak buying periods. For example, many people begin their Christmas shopping as early as September. That is why you start receiving catalogs in the mail. If you are selling something that will coincide with the Christmas season, you will want your mailer to stand out from all the rest. If your item conflicts with holiday purchases, perhaps you should wait until February or send it in the summer, so your piece will be received alone, instead of being lost with all the other mail.

Let me give you an example from a consultant I worked with in south Florida. This gentleman was a competitive runner and wanted to start a track club to train for marathons. Wanting to do a direct mail program to attract members to his club, he followed most of the above advice. However, the timing of his mailing was bad. His offer was to get in shape to run marathons, but it was sent during May. Everyone knows that June though September in south Florida is unbearably hot and humid, and only the most avid runners are on the street. Needless to say, the response was very poor.

The consultant was disappointed, but still wanted to establish his club. I suggested mailing the piece in mid-March to attract members who can begin training in mid-April. Then, when summer comes around, depending on the shape they are in, they can either taper off with their training or continue.

He followed my advice the next year and enrolled eight trainees in his club. He was very happy with the response because, as you know, marathons are not for everyone. I told him that if he plans to use direct mail for his consulting practice, he should always be aware of his timing, his prospects' buying- and decision-making cycles and the economic need for his services.

The moral of this story is to watch your calendar. Send your mailings so they coincide with the known preferred buying cycles of people who would be interested in your products or services.

Principle #6: Make Sense of Your Dollars

This principle of direct mail magic is very simple: Have a budget for the campaign and stick to it. Know how much your list, postage, stationery, printing, overhead and anything else that goes into the campaign will cost. If you cannot afford to conduct a direct mail campaign properly, do not do it at all. Half done is never well done. Never do a mailing on "spec," which is on the hope that enough people will respond to pay for the mailing and make it either pay for itself or somehow be profitable.

Direct mail costs money, and it can also make you a lot of money. It is an investment; like any other investment, if you cannot afford to lose it, do not invest.

I am not trying to discourage you from using direct mail. I am recommending very strongly that you make certain you can afford the campaign if it does not turn out the way you wanted it to. If you have the money, design your budget and stay within it. You can be very successful this way, especially since you are beginning with a small market test.

Principle #7: Have Your Answer Ready

Have your follow-up and fulfillment system in place before you do the mailing. When people respond to your mailing, you may have to answer telephone inquiries, mail brochures or coupons, provide tours, give away freebies, or make presentations to interested respondents. Be totally prepared.

The worst thing you can do is send your mailing and have no way to follow up on it. Fulfillment is critical to the success of your direct mail campaign. People who responded will make requests. They have done exactly as you asked them to do by calling, writing or coming in. If you are not ready for them, you can be sure that they will complain to someone. They will tell their friends how badly they were treated. No small business can afford this negative word-of-mouth. *Make sure you are prepared to answer all the inquiries that come from your direct mail campaign.*

These seven basic principles of direct mail marketing will help you be more successful than if you just take a shotgun approach. Follow these recommendations. Begin with a small test market. As your success grows, expand your mailing areas. Also, check the Appendix for a series of lists on why you should use direct mail and how to further improve your chances of success.

ASK YOURSELF

► Discuss the marketing strategies you are now using that can be improved or enhanced by direct mail.

► Who on your staff has creative or artistic abilities to help you design your direct mail piece? Who else do you have to contact to develop a professional piece and campaign?

► Describe the systems you need in placc to make direct mail work for you.

CHAPTER EIGHT

GET TWICE THE ADVERTISING AT HALF THE COST

FIRE YOUR AD AGENCY

You want me to be more emphatic than that? Never work with an ad agency again. Here are my top seven reasons why.

1. Most ad agencies create an ad campaign, advertising plan or media plan with little or no knowledge or regard for your marketing plan, business or customers.

2. Most ad campaigns are designed to showcase the creative talents of the agencies and win awards for the agency, rather than to increase their clients' sales and revenue. If you doubt this, ask the agency if they are willing to take most or all of their compensation on a contingency, based on a percentage of your increased sales. Most will politely or vigorously decline.

3. Most ad agencies know little or nothing about marketing. Advertising is only one part of marketing, which must complement and support other marketing efforts. Advertising should never be considered a replacement for effective marketing.

4. Traditional advertising, or at least advertising created by most agencies, appears to be based on mass market appeal. As a small business owner, you can never afford to market to the masses. You must target your marketing to specific customers. To learn more about appropriate advertising, read the direct mail ads in magazines. These are more targeted and better written than typical advertisements.

5. If your account is small, you will receive the least amount of attention from the agency, and you will be serviced by their least skilled and qualified employees and account executives. After all, 15%—standard agency commission—of your small business advertising budget is probably a lot less than the commission on a $1 million budget.

6. Agency copywriters write agency copy. This is feel-good copy to showcase their talents and possibly win awards. You do not need this kind of copywriting. With a little help, you can write better copy than most agency copywriters.

7. No agency in the world can advertise and promote your business as well as you can.

These are the reasons I tell you again to fire your advertising agency. Based on your experiences with ad agencies, you can probably even think of more. You can do as well, and I think even better, by creating your own campaign and working with freelance artists and writers to create the visual and written aspects of your ads. Since you hire them as subcontractors, they pay careful attention to your account and give you superior service. After all, they want your good will, referrals and future business.

My success as a marketing consultant has been based on my marketing orientation, rather than an advertising orientation. I have gone into small businesses and larger companies, reviewed their ad campaigns, made specific, marketing-oriented recommendations, rewrote the copy and turned the ads into pieces that sell the products and services of the businesses.

Advertising must be salesmanship in print, on the radio or on television. Advertising must sell your products and services. Otherwise you are just wasting money. No small business can afford to waste money on unproductive and unprofitable advertising.

Look at your competitors and their ads. Do they look nice? Do they say nice things about their companies? These image advertisements probably do not bring in enough business to pay for the placement of the ad. You cannot, and should not, even try to afford an image-building campaign or institutional advertising. Leave that for the megacorporations with money to burn. You need to make every dollar you spend on communicating with the public generate at least 10 times its cost to be profitable—or at a minimum, be self-liquidating and pay for itself in sales.

Do not get me wrong. I am not against advertising. I am against advertising for the sake of advertising and winning awards, rather than creating sales.

Before you think I am totally down on advertising, you must know that I am down on any advertising that is not direct response and designed to generate sales. There are situations when advertising does work and does generate sales and revenue. You can probably think of many yourself. Remember that these situations usually occur when the ad campaign is based on the company's marketing strategy and supports the marketing and sales efforts geared to a target market.

That is what the rest of this chapter is about: How you can make your advertising twice as effective for much less money than you may be used to paying.

TEN MYTHS ABOUT ADVERTISING

Experience and research has taught us that people believe the following 10 common myths about advertising. However, these beliefs have all been exposed as myths, and now you can learn from other people's mistakes.

1. Advertising must be expensive to be effective.
Nothing can be further from the truth. There are many creative and inventive ways to get free advertising that works. There are also many promotional techniques that can be used as advertising to increase your sales.

2. Advertising is too expensive for the small business owner. You can create very effective advertising campaigns for very little money. Also, you can trade out some of your products or services to ad agencies, writers or artists to help you develop your advertising campaign and to media people for free ad placements.

3. Advertising is what you must do to get business.
Advertising is one of many ways to generate business, but it is not what you must do. In fact, there are many more ways to get business than advertising. All of them involve marketing. The key is to keep the business once you have it.

4. One shot, one big hit ad, is all that is needed.
Advertising is not a one-shot deal. That is why they call it an advertising campaign. It must be developed and used over a

period of time. Furthermore, you must realize that it takes between seven and 21 advertising impressions for a person to remember who you are and what you do. This concept is based on the rule of sevens, which states that a message must be noticed by a potential customer at least seven times before any action is taken. It takes at least three tries to get a customer to notice you in the first place. Therefore, you must make between seven and 21 advertising impressions to start being successful. This is in stark contrast to the single impression that comes from a credible referral source.

5. There is one best advertising approach or method.
Advertising is nothing more than an experiment, a shot in the dark. That is why they test advertisements—to try to predict how people will respond. An ad can look or sound great, everyone involved with its creation may think it's great, the medium you place it in thinks it's great, but the customers do not pay attention to it. Small business owners sometimes get caught in a trap because of their limited ad budgets and decide to put all their money into one approach. That is like investing your life savings in a new company's stock and hoping you will not go broke.

Successful advertising is based on testing, testing and retesting. Furthermore, test results do not always reveal what will happen. Remember the disaster with new Coke?

Aside from that, testing is still the best way to determine your probabilities of success. You must test different advertising mediums, parts of the ad, types of offers and anything else you think might influence the customer to buy from you. Therefore, never put all your eggs—money—in one basket by using one approach. Even if it works for you for a while, do not get lulled into a false sense of security. Try a variety of approaches, see which one works the best for a given target market, then invest more time and money in that approach.

6. Advertising does your work for you. No one can afford to sit back and wait for advertising to work. What do you do if it does not?

Advertising is one of several ways to get business—and it is a passive way. Develop active marketing and advertising techniques that support your passive advertising. Work so that the advertising will also work.

7. Short ad copy is better—more effective—than long copy. This is one of the biggest myths about advertising and direct mail. People will read copy of any length, as long as they are interested in it. Reading interest tends to drop off between 50 and 500 words; if you can keep them interested through two pages of copy, you have them hooked. Some of the most successful ads I have ever seen are four-, eight- and 16-page direct mail letters—ads—to prospects and customers.

People do not read long ads because they are not interested in the content. They do not read them because of a weak headline, poor supporting copy or copy that tells the story of the advertiser without emphasizing any benefits for the reader, listener or viewer. Write all your copy, regardless of whether it is short or long, from the customer's perspective. Consider the features of what you are selling, the advantages to the customer, and the benefits they will receive; then, tell them why they must have your product or service.

8. Advertising generally attracts new customers. Advertising often reminds current or former customers why they should continue to do business with you. Your other marketing and promotional techniques do more than advertising to generate new business. If you take issue with this statement, ask yourself how many ads you see and how many you read when you are glancing through a newspaper or magazine.

9. Advertising is most effective when it is image advertising. Every business wants to project a positive and popular public image. The truth is that most, if not all, small businesses cannot afford an image advertising campaign. Most ads are developed to promote an image rather than to sell a service. Look at your competitors' ads; look at your ads. Do your ads tell people how to contact you, where to go to see you, to buy from you? Are your ads image building, ego enhancing advertising or are they direct-response, call-to-action type ads?

10. Advertising determines the success of a business. Many businesses do no formal advertising and are extremely successful. My own consulting business is a case in point. I never pay for advertising of any kind, anywhere. If you have seen an ad for my books, tapes or consulting services in a magazine or newspaper, it is the result of a tradeout for an article I have written or some work I conducted for the publication. The success of my business is totally dependent on marketing and promotions. The same will hold true for your small business.

I must clarify one other myth about advertising and business success. Many people believe that only good or big or expensive advertising agencies can create successful ads. Forget it. I have deliberately never worked with an agency to create ads for my clients, and you do not have to, either. Audition artists, copywriters or other freelancers that you may need; have them help you develop your ads. The campaigns you create will equal or exceed whatever the agency could have created, and at a fraction of the cost.

Now that we have exposed some of the most common myths about advertising, we will discuss ways to develop successful ads and where to place them.

Your Turn   *Complete the following:*

▶ List the 10 advertising myths you subscribe to now.

▶ How will you prevent your business from falling into the trap of any of these myths in the future?

▶ Identify what you can do right now to improve your ads, especially your newspaper and *Yellow Pages* ads.

DEVELOP MONEY-PRODUCING ADS

The headline is the most important part of an ad. If your headline does not scream a benefit to the reader, why should that person take the time to read the rest of your ad? Too many small businesses, even those working with agencies, advertise with a warm fuzzy headline that looks, sounds or feels nice. It may be cute, a poor attempt at humor or it uses innuendos or double entendres. Headlines like these do not get the reader to continue reading.

Here is a little secret about producing great headlines. Sometimes, you have to write the headline last, after the ad is completed. I review hundreds of ads weekly and find that many of the best headlines are buried in the copy, usually in the third or fourth sentence. Take a look at your ads or your competitors' ads. Where is the greatest and most direct benefits statement? When you find it, make it the headline.

Another way to generate results-oriented, money-producing headlines is to ask yourself these questions: Who is it that you want to buy from you now? Identify your target market and make the headline suit them; direct it right at them. What is it that your target market really wants? Put this benefit in the headline or in a subheadline. How can you support the benefit claims you made in the headline? Write motivating body copy to get the reader to call you or come into your place of business. Then, look at this body copy and see if you have an even better headline hidden in there. If you do, use it.

Before you place an ad, check your headlines and copy with some customers. Ask how they would respond if they saw it in the newspaper, heard it on radio or saw it on television. Is the headline motivating? Does the headline make them want to continue reading or listening or watching to get more information? If they say yes, ask them what else you can do to make the headline even more interesting. If they tell you the headline is not motivating, ask them what would motivate them. Use this as the headline.

If they tell you they like the ad or it is very nice, throw it out. If they ask you where or when they can buy your product or service, you have a winner. Go with it.

Results-oriented, money-producing ads start with a great headline. The headline screams a benefit that is specific to the target market and the copy supports that benefit. Identify a benefit or problem in the headline and give the reader support or a solution in the rest of the ad. Finally, tell them to call now or come in to receive this benefit.

Body Copy

After you write the headline, write the copy of the ad or write the headline last. Avoid the mistake where people try to develop their own ads and begin with a headline that says nothing. Since the headline is buried in the copy, but the headline is not interesting enough to get people to continue reading, no one ever gets to the true benefit behind the ad and no one ever gets motivated enough to buy. Consider writing your copy and then searching it for your headline.

Here is a real life example. A chiropractor wanted to promote a back care program for his patients, in addition to his standard treatment offerings. He purchased several pieces of exercise/rehabilitation equipment for his office and created an ad with the headline "Dr. Jones Now Offers Back Care Training Programs."

Not too exciting, is it? Guess what type of response he got? You are right—the response was minimal.

When he asked me to review and revise the ad to make people want to participate, I found the headline in the third sentence. The new, revised headline was "No More Back Pain." This headline tells back pain sufferers there is relief—a solution—for their problem. The copy told the reader how to do some stretching exercises at home to ease the pain and suffering, how to join the program, how long the training/rehabilitation program lasted, what the participant could expect and how to get in touch with the chiropractor.

I suggested to the doctor that, if he continued to write his own ads, he write the ad before deciding on the headlines. I told him to make certain the copy was very specific and geared directly to the target market he was trying to reach. If he still did not have his headline when he finished writing the ad, he should search the copy for the most powerful benefit statement and use that as the headline.

Some Other, Often Forgotten Points about Ad Copy

You do not always have to follow formal grammatical rules. Copy does not have to be, and should never be, written in perfect sentences. In fact, you may want to consider writing in short, choppy, incomplete sentences. This is how people read the fastest and understand the best. It is also the way we talk. Feel free to leave out punctuation marks such as periods and commas and to use leaders (. . .), ALL CAPS, **bold** or *italics* to emphasize a point.

When appropriate, use cliches. Not enough copywriters use cliches. A cliche creates an image that the reader fully understands. They drive the point home and give the writer a leg up. Cliches help you get quickly to the heart of the matter.

When you write your copy, your only concern will be that the copy be powerful and motivating enough to get someone to respond, call you, come see you, buy from you. To keep the reader involved, use repetition—of the headline, the benefits, the call to action. Do not worry about how the copy looks to your high school or college English teacher.

The ad must be salesmanship in print.

Calls to Action

All ads must have a call to action. The call to action tells the reader to contact you by telephone, mail or in person. Make your call to action as visible—large, bold, unique—and direct as possible. Tell your prospects exactly what they must do to receive the benefits in your ad. You want the reader, listener or viewer to respond to you immediately. Now! Today! Not next week. Make your call to action so powerful it moves the prospect to act.

In print advertising, tell them to call, write or visit in big, bold letters. On radio, use music as background and change it and the tone of the announcer's voice when you are giving your call to action. On television, use graphics and other visuals to emphasize and highlight your call to action.

Coding and Tracking

You must code and track all your advertising. Without coding and tracking, you cannot know where your business is coming from; you will never know if your efforts are effective and successful.

Coding an ad is simple. Place an extension on the telephone number in the ad, and change that extension for every place you run it. Have the respondent call and ask for a specific person, or a specific department by number (e.g., department A333). Attach a coupon to the ad and put an expiration date on the coupon, or use a key that only you understand in an unobtrusive part of the coupon (such as, A101).

Your code helps you track the effectiveness of your advertising. This, then, allows you to determine your return on investment. If advertising is costing you $3,000 a month, but you are only selling $1,500 a month worth of products or services, you are losing half of your advertising investment. Now, do not think that the lost $1,500 can be considered image advertising. Remember that most small businesses cannot afford image advertising. The simple truth is that you are losing money, and if you do not code and track your ads, you will never know this.

When you advertise in several mediums simultaneously, such as newspaper and radio or two newspapers, each ad must have its own code. This is extremely important, especially when the ads are identical. You have to be able to determine exactly how much revenue each placement generates. Then, you can decide if the advertising is cost effective and if you want to continue with it.

Be careful of the coding and tracking trap other small businesses fall into. Coding and tracking takes more effort—not much, but a little bit. Yet people often do not want to expend that effort, so they bypass these vitally important activities. Then when it comes time to evaluate the effectiveness of their marketing and advertising programs, they cannot. That is the trap you must avoid. Code and track everything. This way, you will know if you are getting twice the advertising effectiveness for half the cost.

Here are some other ways for you to double your advertising effectiveness with little or no cost to you.

Per Inquiry or Per Order Advertising

Assuming you can convince the advertising medium of the benefits, this very simple approach to advertising allows you to advertise without paying any money up front. You work with a newspaper, magazine or radio or television station to allow you to pay them on a per inquiry basis. You pay them a specified amount of money for every inquiry—call, visit or letter—you get from your ad, or you pay them on a per order or per sale basis. With per order advertising, you are usually paying a slightly higher fee than with per inquiry, because you have already made the sale. In either case, you will have to do a tremendous job of selling this concept to the advertising medium. Have your facts and figures available to show them they can make more money this way than if you simply paid their advertising costs. Sometimes this approach works when the advertising medium is visionary enough to see the potential; sometimes it does not.

Remnant Space Advertising

Remnant space advertising is a way for you to receive a tremendous amount of newspaper or magazine space or radio or TV air time, at very little cost. Remnant space is ad space or air time that is left over because the media could not sell all of its available time or space, or because a previously contracted advertiser pulled out at the last minute. Newspapers and magazines put filler ads or their own ads in these remnant spaces to avoid holes on the page. Radio and TV stations do the same thing. Just take a look at your local newspaper, listen to your radio and watch your television. Whenever you see them advertising themselves, there is a strong possibility this is remnant space.

Here is a suggestion on how to get remnant space, and get it even cheaper than you normally would. Call your newspaper, radio or TV ad rep. Tell him or her that you want to advertise, but you will only use remnant space. The rep may tell you they do not sell remnant space, and you have to pay full price. What the rep says does not matter.

Follow up your phone call with a letter to the rep, or even better, send it to the advertising manager. Explain in the letter that you want to purchase a specific amount of remnant space at 50% or 75% off the rate card price. With the letter, enclose a check and a camera ready copy of your ad.

Make sure your letter states a specific closing date on your offer, such as the thirtieth of the month. Ask the advertising manager either to cash your check when the placement is made, at which time a tear sheet—copy of the printed ad—or tape should be sent to you, or the manager should return your check and your camera ready copy.

Think about the potential of this method of buying ad space. Magazines do not like to have holes in them any more than newspapers do. So, you can call up a national magazine that would normally cost thousands, maybe hundreds of thousands of dollars to advertise in, and tell them you will take their remnant space at a significant discount. All they have to do is call you and you will overnight express a check and camera-ready copy of your ad to them, for inclusion in their magazine.

You might want to design your ad or sales letter, create your camera-ready copy and cut your check in advance, then mail the package to your newspaper or magazine of choice and see what happens. Based on your budget, do the same for radio and TV. Tell them to run your ad or commercial and cash the check if the space becomes available by a certain date. If not, have them send everything back to you.

You are taking an assumptive position here, regardless of whether or not the medium allows remnant space advertising. You are giving them the money up front, albeit at a significant discount from their rate card. The only question now is, does the advertising medium want the cash in hand or will they choose to hold out and hope for a full-paying advertiser?

You can also check out newspapers, magazines, radio and television for ads about themselves. Since these self-promotions are probably remnant space ads, call and ask if they will accept an offer on future remnant space.

If they do, great. You will get more than twice the advertising value you are paying for. If they do not accept remnant space ads, you can motivate them to start accepting these ads with yours as the first one.

OTHER ADVERTISING APPROACHES

Everyone wants to be a star or at least achieve their 15 minutes of fame. I have never met a true entrepreneur who did not want to be a guest on a radio or television show, write a column for a newspaper or magazine or star in a video. Now you can have all these things as part of your advertising program, and none of them has to cost you an arm and a leg.

A Star Is Born, or How I Made It in Home Movies

Many businesses, both large and small, use videos as marketing tools. These brief video resumes or sales presentations are very eye-catching and convincing to a customer. You can have your own professional video for a very reasonable cost. The video can describe your business, your customer service policies, the benefits your customers receive from doing business with you and anything else you can think of.

You can show the video in your store or office, at trade shows or mall expositions, at chamber of commerce meetings or other civic meetings and anywhere else that people would want to see and learn about your business. You can be a star and help your business grow at the same time.

If you are adventuresome and want to go beyond home or professional corporate videos, you can star in your own television show. There are two simple ways to do this. Either produce your own show and buy the time on a television station, much like the infomercials do, or contact a TV station and see if they are interested in producing a show with you as the host. When you make your sales presentation to the station, remember to focus on the benefits to the viewer and the station. Your business will benefit simply by you being the host of the show.

If the local network affiliates do not have a time slot for you, consider cable television. Most cable stations are looking for a local business or how to show. Work out the costs with the station manager, but first see if they will produce the show for free and sell advertising for you. Find out if you can sell your products or services and even those of your guests on the show. If the station will not fund the show, ask if the revenues from the sales can be used to pay for the air time. Ask if you can sell advertising for the show and keep the differential of your price from the station price, plus the 15% agency placement commission. This is a neat little way for you to make extra money while airing your own television show.

Maybe you do not want to star in your own video or TV show. That is okay. Position yourself as an expert so you can appear on other people's shows. When they have you as a guest, your expertise and credentials are highly promoted. Viewers will want to do business with you, or at least contact you. Just make sure you give them a reason to call you as soon as you get off the show.

This same advice holds true for a radio show. Be a guest on as many talk shows as you can, on as many different stations. If you have your own show and you can do this by purchasing the time from the station, make certain you have listeners call in with questions or to request a free product or service. Remember to mention your products and services several times during your show or interview and to tell the listeners how they can get in touch with you. Mention your phone number at least three times every five minutes.

Brochures

Brochures are an excellent way to advertise your small business, depending on what you are selling. Brochures are a take-along or leave-behind piece in which people can read about your products or services. Therefore, when you are not there the brochure must sell for you.

Do not fall into the trap of writing your own brochure. Experience has shown that business owners and other technical professionals are experts in their field, but they are not expert copywriters. When they write a brochure, they tend to write it as a me-too piece, an ego enhancer or a technical or informational report. Your brochure must be a sales piece, written to and for customers. It must extol the benefits they will receive when they do business with you. Above all, your brochure must constantly sell for you when you are not there. The repetition here is deliberate, to drive home the point.

Hire professional marketing experts to help you write and develop your brochure. Allow these consultants to hire and direct the artists, printers and writers who will work on your brochure. Leave it up to them to turn your concepts into a sales tool. Then pay attention to the business of running your business while they create your masterpiece.

Consider the following when you develop your brochure.

► Who is your audience?

► What are you trying to sell them?

► What layout, design, copy and artwork will best communicate your message to them?

► What type of budget is available to produce the brochure?

► Will the brochure be black and white, one, two, three or four colors? Will it have pictures and/or illustrations?

► How will the brochure be used: as a handout, a mailer, a take along or a leave behind?

► Will the brochure help or hurt your business?

After you answer these seven questions, you are ready to begin work on your brochure. One other recommendation: if you hire a copywriter to write the brochure, get that person to agree to provide you with at least two written revisions within the price they quote you for the project. Remember, they are taking your ideas and putting them into words that will sell. If you are not happy with the way their copy reads, reserve the right to make changes. Two revisions are fair. After that, you should pay the copywriter for additional time.

Fliers, Data Sheets and Fact Sheets

Fliers, data sheets and fact sheets are one-page brochures. Fliers announce office or store openings, special events, programs and unique service offerings. A flier must sell the audience—the marketplace—on what you are selling. When you create a flier, follow the same rules you use for creating an ad. Make your headline attention-getting. Use graphics, pictures, motivating phrases and a call to action on every flier. Your call to action should include both a coupon with your business name and address and, separately, your telephone number.

Like brochures, fliers can be printed in two, three or four colors. This can get expensive. You can achieve a similar effect by using colored paper instead of white. Gold, royal blue and some of the neon colors definitely attract attention, even when the flier is printed in black ink. In fact, print only in black ink when you use colored paper. It makes it easier to read.

Be as original as you want with your fliers. There are no limitations. The purpose of your flier is to attract attention to some event or sale; how you do that is to your credit. Since you will want to track the effectiveness of your fliers, code them. Even though fliers are an inexpensive advertising technique, you will be pleasantly surprised at the results they bring.

Electronic Media

There is a proliferation of on-line computer bulletin boards. Some of the more well known include CompuServe, Prodigy, GEnie, Dialogue and Delphi. There are also local bulletin boards through computer users groups right in your own city. Find one that you can become a member of, let the other people know who you are and what you do and ask if you can advertise on the board. Using this technique, there is a good chance you can gain a large number of new customers. In fact, many consultants and small home-based businesses have gotten started just by advertising on computer bulletin boards.

Electronic billboards are another advertising method you can use. These flashing messages change every minute or so, and yours is placed in a rotation. This is different from a standard outdoor billboard where your message stays fixed for the contracted period of time. The electronic billboard does capture people's attention, especially motorists who are either passing by or stuck at a traffic light. You may want to check into these costs as an alternative advertising method.

If you have an office or storefront, consider electronic moving displays. These are like mini electronic billboards, where the message rolls across the screen, except that the message is always promoting your business.

You will be surprised at how many people stop in front of a window to read an electronic message display. Try one for yourself. See if it brings you the customers you are looking for.

Promotions

Promotions are more of a support technique or a traffic builder than a true advertising technique. However, since the purpose of a promotion is to stimulate business and communicate a message to the public, it is included here with the other advertising techniques.

When you stage a promotion, you are trying to increase sales in a short period of time. You are doing something, perhaps offering a discount or a two for one sale to make more people buy what you are selling and to draw attention to your business.

The following list includes 10 of the best and most successful types of promotions that you should consider using to stimulate sales for your business.

1. *Sampling*—giveaways of your products or services

2. *Discounts*—lower your prices for a specified time or give customers two for the price of one

3. *Specialty Items*—key chains, mugs, calendars, bags, pens, logo watches, shirts, caps, etc.

4. *Contests*—a great way to start an in-house mailing list; remember, there must be a winner

5. *Premiums*—specialty items used as value-added incentives to purchase, which help to expand your business

6. *Seminars and Speeches*—talk to your prospects where they work, where you work, and wherever you can meet

7. *Frequent Buyer Cards or Stamp Plans*—get enough holes punched in your card or collect enough stamps to get something for free

8. *Coupons*—two for one, discounts, free reports, special sales to your best customers, or anything else

9. *Exhibitions*—show the public what you have

10. *Referral Building*—customer get a customer program with recognition and reward programs for the referral source

Use any or all of these promotional techniques properly and you will experience a short-term increase in sales. Then it is up to you to stay in touch with your new customers and keep them happy so they will continue to buy from you.

You can create combinations of these promotional techniques or create totally new techniques. Whatever you do, sales promotions are a great way to boost your revenues and support your advertising and marketing programs.

How You Can Mail Everything for Free

You can mail your advertising message, flier, brochure, coupon or other direct mail piece for free. In fact, you can mail them and make money on the postage. Here is how.

You are no doubt familiar with the co-op or marriage mailer companies and programs, such as Val-Pak, Advo, Money Mailer and Stuff-It. These direct mail companies sell you a coupon or flier in their mailing package for several hundred dollars and guarantee that your piece, along with about 20 others, will be mailed to 10,000 or 20,000 residents in your business service area. If you have ever received one of these packets, you know that the host company has an ad in there, too. And what do you think it cost them? Nothing!

Here is how to cut out the middle man, regardless of whether you do a mailing to residents or businesses. Identify the target market you want to reach. Then find out the costs of the mailing list, stuffing the envelopes, printing and the postage. When you have your total costs, go to noncompeting businesses and tell them you will do the mailing and printing for them if they provide you with camera-ready copy. Give them a price that covers these costs and leaves enough over to cover your contribution costs to the package.

For example, if a 5,000-piece mailing will cost you $5,000, including postage, printing and stuffing, go to 10 or 20 businesses. Sell them on your mailing packet. Have them pay you either $500 or $250 each to be a part of your program, or charge them slightly more and make a profit for your efforts.

This program takes some effort on your part, but the rewards are tremendous. Imagine mailing all your marketing pieces for free every time you want to contact prospects or customers.

GETTING MORE BUSINESS TO COME TO YOU

These final thoughts about advertising are provided to remind, enlighten and motivate you to consider and reconsider everything you do to communicate with the buying public. Some of these suggestions repeat what has already been said in this chapter; others provide new ideas or expand upon old ones. Consider each recommendation and how it will help business come to you. Use it as it is or adapt it however you see fit to make your advertising twice as effective at half the price. Also, check the Appendix for several more advertising suggestions.

1. *All advertising must be direct response.* If you do not get a response, how will you know if your advertising is working? How will you make more sales? How will you track the ad's effectiveness?

2. *Code all ads to track them.* While this is easy for print ads, you can still code radio and TV ads. Just have the caller ask for a specific person or a particular extension. That will tell you which ad or commercial the contact came from.

3. *Every ad, printed or commercial, must have a headline that screams a benefit and arouses interest.* People are most interested in what your product or service can do for them. Your headline catches their interest by providing the initial answer to their question *WIIFM*—What's in It for Me? Your copy then supports your headline and continues to answer the question.

4. *Subheads and body copy must always support the headline.* This extends recommendation 3. You may even want to write your copy first. Your best headline is often found in one of the first three or four sentences. If your copy seems to be repetitive where benefits are concerned, good. It should be. You must drive home the reasons why customers should buy from you.

5. *All advertising must be created from the customer's pers-pective.* Never create me-too ads, telling how great you are and all the wonderful things you and your business have done. Your customers couldn't care less, unless you tell them exactly what you have accomplished for another customer. Specific benefit and results informa-tion will arouse their interest. Find out what your cus-tomers need and want, and tell them in your ads how you will give it to them better than anyone else can.

6. *Use a features-advantages-benefits chart to help create your advertising.* People know a great deal about the features, but have a difficult time translating these features into advantages and benefits. Create a three-column chart. Head the columns Features, Advantages and Benefits. For each feature, describe why it is advantageous for a customer to do business with you and the benefits they will receive from this relationship.

7. *Advertising must support the overall marketing plan.* No amount of small business advertising in the world can save a poor marketing plan. It is a waste of money, unless, of course, you have unlimited funds and can keep advertising in the hope of generating business based on your image. Unfortunately, most small businesses do not have these kinds of funds. Therefore, create a workable and doable marketing plan and develop your advertising to support that plan.

8. *Never do image advertising.* It is too expensive for your small business and it sells nothing. If it does not sell, it does not generate customers and revenue. If you have no customers and no revenue, you have no business.

9. *Learn about the psychology of selling and advertising.* Customers have fears that your advertising can address. Tell them how you can help them put these fears aside. Show them how you can reduce their anxieties and help them solve their problems. When your ads address their fears, anxieties, concerns and problems, and you offer

resolutions, you will find more people doing business with you and more people referring business to you.

10. *Never overpromise anything in your ads and then under-deliver.* It is always better to underpromise and over-deliver. When you give people more than they expect, they perceive they have received extra value for their purchase. They are more satisfied with the way you do business. In fact, this principle is one of the mainstays of successful customer service.

11. *Make sure you can live up to any guarantees you advertise.* Offer customers a guarantee. This relieves any anxieties or concerns they may have about buying from you. Whatever your guarantee is, whether it is money-back, free replacements, or anything else, live up to your guarantee exactly as you advertise it. If you do not, you can expect negative word-of-mouth and publicity from dissatisfied customers. You may even get a call from the Better Business Bureau or some other agency.

12. *Be different, creative, innovative and off the wall.* Do not do everything the way your competitors do it. Make yourself stand out from the crowd. Be outrageous. Be different. Do not be shy about anything you do that does not take the standard approach. Different sells and attracts customers, as long as the creative and different approach is in good taste.

13. *Do not use large ad agencies.* Use consultants and freelancers to help create your marketing programs and ad campaigns. The results will be as good, the quality of the work will be as high and you will receive a great deal of personal attention. Your account is probably too small for the ad agency to place one of their senior people on it, and you will have to pay them a 15% commission or an upcharge on their work. You can save these costs by using freelancers, with whom you can interact daily and control the development of your advertising materials.

14. *Never use advertising in place of a personal meeting or contact.* People buy from people, not from or because of ads. Advertising is a support vehicle, not a replacement selling vehicle. Advertising must be salesmanship in print, but it should never take the place of a sales person or a face-to-face meeting. If you can sell to someone personally, do it. Never substitute advertising for direct contact.

15. *Give ads a chance.* Design your advertising program to support your marketing program. Do not pull the ads after one or two placements or because they are not yet generating the responses you are looking for. Give ads a chance to be recognized by your prospects and customers. Allow them to work for you. Do not panic. Remember that you are working within an advertising budget and a media schedule.

    If the ads are not working, change the headline, some of the copy, the offer or the call to action. See if this revised ad does better. Only when you have exhausted your possibilities, based on testing and tracking, or spent your budget, should you pull the campaign.

There you have it. These are some of the best suggestions on how to make your advertising twice as effective, how to make it twice as successful, and how to get twice the advertising at half the price. Remember to develop your advertising plan from the marketing plan, set the plan in motion and give it a chance to work. Then track its effectiveness. If, after a certain amount of time, you are not seeing the results you expected or desired, it is time to change the advertising program. Check your research, target markets, messages and everything else you were using to communicate with prospects and customers. Revise the ads, implement new ones and give the new campaign a chance to work.

You want your advertising to generate business for you as soon as possible. If it cannot do this immediately, your advertising should at least generate interest in your business. Each marketing activity must either generate a sale or move the prospect one step closer to a sale. Once the interest is there, it is up to you and your staff to convert interested prospects into customers.

One last thought. Be consistent in your advertising and marketing messages. Do not jump around with different slogans, pitches and phrases. The more consistent you are, the more people will recognize your business, what it does and what you stand for. As an example, a clothing store provides personal wardrobe consulting for free, while every other store either charges for it or does not even offer it. Any ad should state these unique messages every time, all the time: The personal wardrobe consulting is free. Repeat the message until customers identify it with your business. Continuity and consistency of your messages help to make your advertising and marketing twice as effective.

ASK YOURSELF

► How much of your advertising is image-centered rather than selling-oriented?

► How can you turn the features of your product or service into benefits—advantages, solutions—for your customers?

► What type of coding and tracking system must you develop? How can you improve your current system?

► Are your ads producing enough revenue to make them self-liquidating, where the revenue offsets the cost of the ads?

► Is your ad copy company-oriented or customer-oriented?

  • Is it feature rich or benefit rich?

  • What changes or improvements must you make?

CHAPTER NINE

DO'S AND DON'T'S
OF MEDIA
PLACEMENT

AD PLACE-MENT

Most small businesses tend to advertise in newspapers; some add radio and television in certain situations. Which is right for your business, and when should you choose a particular advertising medium?

While each type of advertising has its benefits and drawbacks, consider several things before you make ad placements or begin an ad campaign.

▶ What is your advertising budget?

▶ Who is your target audience?

▶ What is the best advertising medium for you to use to reach your target audience?

▶ What are your response capabilities to make a sale if a customer comes in, or to fulfill an information request that you receive in writing or over the phone?

▶ And what, exactly, are your marketing/advertising goals?

You are not limited to advertising in only one medium at a time. If your budget permits it, you can run your ad in multiple mediums, such as newspapers and radio. If you do this, it will have a definite affect on your selection of placements. The primary reason will be the cost factor associated with multiple and simultaneous placements. On the other hand, if you can afford it, you can use multiple advertising mediums to support each other and increase your overall effectiveness.

Print Advertising

Print advertising has several advantages. Since most small businesses advertise in their local newspaper, the lists of advantages and disadvantages will pertain specifically to newspapers.

Some of the advantages are:

1. The ad lasts longer than radio and television.

2. People can go back and read it.

3. You can put a coupon in it that they have to cut out and bring to you.

4. It can be fairly affordable, especially small display or classified ads.

5. You can reach a large audience at one time.

6. You can select specific sections of the paper to advertise in.

7. Your local newspaper has acceptance and credibility with the reading public.

Be aware, however, that if your business is located in a city where there is only one major newspaper, that paper can charge you and everyone else higher than normal rates because they have no competition. If this is the case, take a look at the smaller neighborhood papers and see if these will reach your target markets.

The disadvantages of print advertising include:

1. You do not know how many people read your ad. Do not believe the paper's circulation numbers. While they may sell that many papers, you can be sure that all the buyers are not reading your ad. In fact, research says people only see ads they are consciously or subconsciously looking for. If that is the case, most readers of a newspaper will never even see your ad.

2. Print advertising is sold on a space basis. The more advertisers that compete for that space, the higher the costs of the ad. This is especially true if your local paper has no competition. You could be caught in what appears to be price gouging, and there would be nothing you could do about it.

3. The number of ads in your paper reduces the impact of your ad. This has nothing to do with size or position. It is strictly a function of numbers. You have to overcome this clutter effect by writing killer copy, using creative borders on your ad, such as dashes to make it look like a coupon, or getting your ad placed on the front page of a section.

4. No matter how large the circulation, you can never reach your entire potential market with one newspaper.

5. If you do not catch a reader's eye immediately, they may throw the paper out and not remember your ad. Newspapers count on this and it is why they try to sell you frequency placements. This is good for them if they can sell it, and it may or may not be bad for you if you can afford it. The more times people see your ad, the more likely they are to do business with you.

6. Unless your ad is powerful and direct response oriented, it will not create action on the part of the buyer. Check out the ads in your local paper. Most of them are image ads, and frankly, you cannot afford to do that.

7. Local events can decrease the response to your ads. This is especially true if the local events receive editorial coverage. Written articles—editorials—are read 50% more of the time than ads. Since it is already difficult to get someone to read your ad in all the clutter, think how much more difficult it becomes with editorial coverage of local events.

BUYING AD SPACE

Display or space ads are based on column inches. This means that your ad will be a certain number of columns wide by a certain number of inches long. Multiply the two numbers to get your column inches. Newspapers have a rate for each column inch. The price is then calculated according to that rate times your column inches.

Your costs on display advertising and even classified advertising can decrease by asking for a contract rate. A contract rate means you will place a minimum specified number of column inches with the paper during the year. The more inches of advertising you will place, the better your rate will be.

Here are some other things you need to understand and several questions you need to ask when you are negotiating your contract rate. What happens if you do not use up all the space you contract for? Are you liable for not fulfilling the contract, and will you have to pay the higher prevailing rate for using a lesser number of inches? Are you required to use a small classified ad as a rate holder? This type of ad is placed by you on a daily or weekly basis; it costs you money and guarantees the paper will maintain your contract rate for you. Get this information before you sign any advertising contracts. You do not want to be surprised when you receive an invoice that is higher than you expected.

Let the Paper Help You

Here are some other suggestions. Newspapers do not require camera-ready ads or artwork. They are more than happy to typeset and lay out your ads for you, for free. Avail yourself of these free typesetting and layout services. Newspapers also have graphic artists and copywriters who will help you create your ad, again for free. While I recommend the free type-setting and layout services, I strongly caution you about the free artists and writers. Most times you will get what you pay for. Besides, nobody can write your ads as well as you can.

A final thought on print advertising. Ask for a proof copy of your ad before it runs in the paper and for tear sheets. Tear sheets are the actual newspaper pages on which your ad was run. The proof allows you to see the ad before it runs; the tear sheet allows you to see it as it looks to the reader when it runs. These requests will guarantee your ad looks the way you want it to look and that it was placed on the day and in the section you requested.

Track responses to your ads. Use the best one as a control, which means you will test other ads against this one to see which creates the best response. Keep all of them to help you improve your future ads.

Your Turn **List the advantages and disadvantages of print advertising to you and your business.**

RADIO ADVERTISING

Although it may be hard to believe, in some markets radio advertising is less expensive than print advertising. If this is true where you live, strongly consider radio as your advertising medium of choice.

The same principles hold true for radio ads as for print ads. You must have an interesting and attention-getting headline, the ad must tout all your customer's benefits, the copy must support the headline and promote the benefits, the ad must always be selling and providing calls to action.

Additionally, you have another medium, sound, in which to get your message across. Use this to your advantage. Have the announcer modulate the tone and rate of his or her voice and vary the pitch. These changes in the voice will always catch the attention of the listener. That is why automobile ads tend to speak quickly and loudly, to get your attention. Do whatever you must to get the listener's attention. You have only 15, 30 or 60 seconds.

Radio advertising representatives will also talk to you about reach (how many people listen to a show), frequency (how often they listen) and gross rating points or GRP (the multiple of reach and frequency). Do not worry about these terms. Instead, think of the following.

Does the station/show I want to advertise on have enough listeners in the age/income/demographic bracket that I want to reach to warrant spending my money with them? If your answer is yes, ask to see their numbers from the rating services, not their own research. You want hard proof that you will be able to reach the people you need to reach. Going on an ad rep's say is not enough justification for spending your hard-earned money, even though the rep is probably telling the truth.

When you have decided to advertise on radio, select your show or times. Specific times usually cost you more than run of schedule (ROS), which is where they put your ad on the radio whenever they have unsold time. If you are a 24-hour business, this may not be so bad, because most unsold time is available in the middle of the night. This time costs less so you can get more for your money, and these listeners are the night owls you are trying to attract to your business.

Work with the rep to select your times. Then have the station prepare a media buy for you. The media buy shows you the dates, times, name of the show, length of commercial/ad, and number of ads you will have during a specific time period. The buy also shows your costs and when you are expected to pay. If the station has a sophisticated computer system, the printout of the buy will also show the reach, frequency and gross rating points of each show your commercial will be on.

Once you have agreed to place your ads, negotiate the cost. It is very rare that ad reps stick to the rate card. Ask how much the price per ad can be reduced if you run more commercials. Find out the difference in costs if your entire buy is based on run of schedule. Discuss the possibility of the station giving you unsold time on the more popular shows at reduced prices. These are all ways to get more for your radio advertising dollar.

After you have completed these negotiations, ask the station to match your paid ads with free ads, plus promotional one-liners. The free ads are your commercials run at various times of the day, either as sold spots or during unsold time. The liners are usually 10- to 30-second commercials read live by the host or disc jockey or played on tape that promote your business. They are free.

If you get free matching ads, you will probably not be able to specify when they run. Just the fact that they will run has effectively doubled your advertising. Another way to increase the effectiveness of your ads is to tell the station to call you whenever they have unsold air time. You may want to have them air your commercial. This is the same as remnant space in print advertising. The concept is not often used by small business on radio or TV, but you can be the first. With remnant or unsold space, you could possibly negotiate a tremendously favorable price for yourself. You never know until you ask or offer.

By now, I can see you worrying about production costs and voice talent. Do not worry. Radio stations are glad to produce your commercials for free, as long as you buy a specific amount of time with them. They can also help you with the scripts and provide the talent for the voices. This saves you a lot of money. All you have to do is ask them for this service.

Remember, though, you must receive a tape proof of the commercial before it airs. This is like your ad proof from a newspaper. Make certain the commercial says what you want it to say, in the way you want it said. This is especially important if the talent was supplied by the station. If the words are incorrect or the commercial does not sound right to you, have the station redo it.

Here are the advantages and disadvantages of radio advertising.

Advantages

1. Most households have radios.

2. Adults listen to radio at least three hours a day.

3. Radio can reach a more targeted audience than newspapers.

4. Radio is everywhere, as most cars also have radios.

5. Radio is an active medium, since people are listening to your commercial. Therefore, your radio ad can create a demand for your product or service.

6. The auditory message is easily remembered.

7. Radio commercials and disc jockey promotions make the public perceive you as an expert or authority.

8. Your credibility is enhanced, especially when a host reads your commercial.

Disadvantages

1. Prime time, drive time and popular programs are expensive.

2. Your ads are limited by what you can communicate with sound.

3. Although your ads can create a demand, listeners cannot usually respond immediately. That is why you must make it easy and memorable for them to respond.

4. Listeners punch buttons, just as TV remote control addicts zap during commercials. You may lose your audience.

5. If your small business provides a limited range of products or services, the audience your radio commercial reaches may be too broad and, therefore, not cost effective.

6. Unless your radio ad is direct response, and most are not, there is no way to track its effectiveness. You need to provide the listener with a method to respond, even though they may not respond immediately, and a code to respond to, so you can track your commercials.

TELEVISION ADVERTISING

Television advertising is expensive. There are no two ways about it. It costs more than $300,000 to air a 60-second commercial on today's most popular television shows. Obviously, it costs a lot less on other shows. Is TV advertising worth it? That depends on what you are trying to achieve.

While television reaches the greatest amount of people in the least amount of time, you pay for that premium and capability. Production costs must be added to your time costs. Network advertising and specialty shows or events like the Super Bowl are more expensive than local station advertising. Cable TV is less expensive than all of them.

Stations may sometimes work with you to produce your television commercial. If you buy enough time, they may provide a film crew for you and charge you a reduced rate, but you may have to hire your own film crew and pay the prevailing rate. In any case, TV commercials can be expensive to produce. Remember the Nike commercial with Bugs Bunny and

Michael Jordan that aired at the 1992 NBA All Star game? Reports place the cost of making that commercial, not airing it, at around $3 million. That is an unbelievable amount of money for a short time on a television screen.

On the other side of the coin, though, you have probably seen television commercials, especially on cable TV, that show still pictures or graphics with a voice over or one person sitting on a desk or chair talking to the camera. These are relatively inexpensive to produce. The key is the quality of the film and the message in the commercial, and this is what determines whether people watch your ad.

If you choose television as an advertising medium, make your commercials as inviting, exciting and motivating as possible. Show your business and employees having a great time servicing customers. Use colors, fast-changing scenes, music and lots of visuals. Show activity. Activity breeds activity. Let the viewer see happy customers. Use their testimonials. These create credibility and overcome viewer skepticism faster and easier than anything else you can do on a commercial. Be sure to give the telephone number and address of your business at least two or three times during the commercial.

Once you have decided to run television commercials, have the station create a media buy for you. Ask them to match your paid commercials with free commercial time. If they have unsold air time, they may be willing to put you on. Also, to save money, consider ROS with TV just as with radio. If you do not think people are awake watching in the middle of the night—the most unsold commercial time is still here, just as in radio—consider that infomercials got their start in the middle of the night, with the products for night owls and insomniacs. Now, infomercials are a multibillion dollar a year business; you never know who is watching your commercial, so do not negate run of schedule placements.

Another approach is to have the station edit your 30- or 60-second commercial to 10 or 15 seconds, use that as a filler when they have unsold time. You have seen this done by other advertisers. It is the same commercial, only shorter. Just make sure the basic message still gets to the viewer and they still have a way to contact you.

You never know if you can get these extra placements unless you ask. Here are some advantages and disadvantages of television advertising.

Advantages

1. TV targets viewers by program interest and can therefore give you specific information on their characteristics.

2. TV reaches the most people in the least amount of time.

3. It is the most visible and visual medium for advertising and can show off your products or service like no other method.

4. Because it is a visual medium, you can be more creative with a television commercial than with any other type of ad.

5. Your business achieves a high degree of credibility from advertising on television.

6. Cable TV is relatively low cost, especially if you advertise on the bulletin board channels or public access.

7. Some stations will put you on their talk shows if you are an advertiser with them. This helps your image and raises public awareness about your small business.

Disadvantages

1. TV is the most expensive advertising medium today.

2. You cannot control the zapping, and therefore, your commercial may never get seen.

3. Production costs can be very expensive; they sometimes exceed the cost of airing the commercial.

4. Although the statistical data from the station and the rating services gives you an idea of who might be watching a particular show, you can never be sure.

YELLOW PAGES ADVERTISING

Your business will receive a free listing in the *Yellow Pages,* just for having a business phone. *Yellow Pages* reps will try to sell you larger display ads or in-column ads. Be aware that these cost, and if you decide to go with a larger ad, your *Yellow Pages* display ad better be bringing in 10 times its monthly costs in revenues. Otherwise, the ad is not effective and becomes a cash drain.

If you feel you need a larger ad than the one line listing, consider working with your in-column ad before you consider a display ad. Make the in-column ad bolder, use larger lettering, use red ink (maybe), use a logo, or develop an eye-catching, in-column display ad. This will stand out when the reader gets to your page. It is also less expensive than regular display ads.

Here is a quick and easy way to make your in-column display ad stand out, regardless of how many display ads are on your page. Put dashes around your ad, as a border. Somewhere in the ad, include the word free in bold, capital letters. People will be drawn to your dashes and the word free.

Be creative with your *Yellow Pages* ad. Think about writing the ad as an editorial or article. Remember that articles and editorials are read 50% more of the time than ads. It is your creativity, the appearance and the content of the ad that will get it read, not necessarily the size.

The *Yellow Pages* places their ads alphabetically, by category and then name. First come full-page ads in a category, then half-page, and so on down the line until there are no more display ads. That is why they tell you they want to sell you a large display ad: so you can be closer to the front of your category. Do not believe it. Full page display ads are not necessarily for everyone. It depends on your type of business and what you are selling in the ad.

If you use a display ad, follow the principles for print advertising, where your headline screams a benefit. Add a banner headline in reversed out print—white print on a black background—that gives away something for free. It can be a pamphlet, a sample product, a service or anything else you can think of. This captures the reader's attention and gets them to continue reading your ad.

The rest of your ad talks about problems and solutions and benefits to the reader. Try not to list features or program/ service names. List the benefits they will receive when they buy your product or service. Make your telephone number stand out and be sure your business name is readable. Never make your name the headline or the largest part of the ad, like so many businesses do. People are not interested in your business name or location or how they can reach you until they know you can satisfy some need they have right now. In fact, this advice holds true for every type of ad. Get people to read about your benefits and problem solutions, and then lead them to your telephone number, name and location.

You can have your *Yellow Pages* ad prepared for free by the company that is selling you the advertising. They will lay it out, design it, typeset it and show you as many proofs as you desire before it is printed. Again, all this work costs you nothing. It is free. Just ask for it, and they will gladly provide the service. Always keep in mind, though, that you might get what you pay for.

When your ad appears in the *Yellow Pages,* you may be contacted by a *Yellow Pages* buying service. They will tell you that they can place your ads for you at a cheaper rate than you are paying now. Be careful. Check this out by calling the *Yellow Pages* directly and getting price quotes on the same size ads. Often, the buying service does not really save you any money. They may offer you a discount if you pay them in full (e.g., 10% off when the entire year is paid in full), but this may be your only savings. Determine if this is worth having your cash in their account, or if you would rather pay the full amount of the ad directly to the *Yellow Pages,* on a monthly basis. This way, over the course of the year, your money is still working for you.

The following suggestion about *Yellow Pages* advertising is made by many authors and "experts," but I have never been convinced of its true effectiveness.

People often read a category from the beginning. Since listings are placed in alphabetical order, they recommend you start your business name with an *A,* or as many *A*s as possible. It may work some of the time, but I am not certain you have to change your business name or create one that places you first in the category. If your advertisement is creative and fulfills a need for the reader, customers will call you.

One other point about *Yellow Pages* advertising involves color—specifically red. The reps will tell you that by using red, either in your one line listing or in a display ad, your inquiries will increase. They will even show you data and statistics to support this claim.

Ask them about the other advertisers who use red, but never see an increase in their calls. Again, I believe that it is not the red color that gets people to call you; it is the content of your ad and the fact that you are offering a solution to a problem they have. Remember, of all the ways to reach an interested and motivated buyer, the *Yellow Pages* is the best; when a person opens that book, they are ready to make a call or visit your place of business. Now that you have them interested, you have to sell them and keep them as customers.

ASK YOURSELF

► What is your advertising budget?

► Who is your target audience?

► Discuss the best advertising medium for you to use to reach your target audience.

► Describe your response capabilities to make a sale if a customer comes in, or to fulfill an information request.

► Elaborate on your marketing/advertising goals.

CHAPTER TEN

HOW TO SELL YOUR PRODUCTS AND SERVICES

SELLING IS NOTHING MORE THAN EFFECTIVE COMMUNI-CATION

Marketing your small business is a lot of fun. You get to do so many interesting things as you get the word out about who and what you are. Once you inform the public about your products and services, you must sell to them.

Selling is perceived by many people as a dirty word. Yet, all of us sell something all the time. To be a successful sales person, you have to have the right attitude. Knowing the technicalities of selling helps, but you can be just as successful, and sometimes more successful, if you just apply yourself to the cause of getting someone to buy what you are selling.

Before I knew the technicalities of successful selling, I was a successful salesperson. All I did was try to communicate honestly and effectively with people. When you ask the right questions, listen carefully for the answers, and then focus your presentation to provide solutions to the problems you uncovered in the prospect's answers, you cannot help but be a successful salesperson.

That is why I say that selling is nothing more than effective communication.

The Appendix includes some lists and charts about communication techniques and interpersonal skills that will make your selling infinitely easier, regardless of whether you sell a product or service. For now, let me provide you with a basic primer on selling. We will go through the steps together and see how to make them work.

If you are in retail, at first you may not see the value of some of these steps to successful selling. However, remember that where a service provider must prospect to get clients, you too must prospect to get customers. Although your prospecting may be different, such as advertising or promotions, there are many similarities between a retail product salesperson and a services salesperson.

SEVEN BASIC STEPS TO SUCCESSFUL SELLING

The seven basic steps to successful selling are *prospecting, qualifying, scheduling the appointment, making the presentation, handling objections, closing the sale* and *servicing the customer.* Literally hundreds, if not thousands of books are dedicated to some or all of these aspects of selling. Following is a summary of each and how you can use your skills to become a more successful salesperson.

Step 1. Prospecting

The only way you can make a sale is to find a customer. And, the only way to find a customer is to prospect. To make a sale, you have to generate leads to be followed up.

Prospecting can occur in any number of ways. You can offer people a free sample of what you are selling. You can give a seminar that is free to the public or to invited participants. You can call or mail something to people on a mailing list. You can think of other ways to generate names of people who would be interested in your product or service. Notice how all these suggestions relate to marketing. You might think of prospecting and lead generation as a marketing tactic. If you are afraid of prospecting for sales, this may take some of the sting out of it.

The key to prospecting is getting the right names. There are experts who will tell you that you must get as many names as possible, then qualify them. I will tell you that this is a waste of your time. Why spin your wheels with hundreds or thousands of people who would never buy from you anyway?

When you prospect, get the names of people who will buy your product or service. You can purchase mailing lists, send press releases or articles to specific publications that are read by your desired customers, or give presentations to groups made up of your desired customers. This is marketing, pure and simple—get the names of the people who will buy from you and sell what you have to them.

Step 2. Qualifying Prospects

Not everybody whose name you collect will buy from you, nor is every person a good prospect for your product or service. You must qualify them as someone who needs, wants and can afford what you are selling.

You qualify prospects according to characteristics. These can be demographic characteristics, such as age, income, gender, education, job title, etc. Or, use psychosocial characteristics such as size of family, professional and civic affiliations, schools attended, affinity—membership—groups, etc.

Whatever way you qualify your prospects, the key is to make certain they need and can afford what you are selling. You would not open a jewelry store like Tiffany's in a neighborhood with a total household income of $20,000. However, you might be pleasantly surprised if you opened an upscale flea market in a neighborhood with a median household income of $50,000 or higher.

Just check out the people who you want to be your customers. Qualify them according to the characteristics you decide are the most appropriate, and then try to sell to them.

Step 3. Scheduling the Appointment

A service provider, such as a stock broker, financial planner, and yes, a marketing consultant, must work to schedule an appointment with a qualified prospect. Other books will tell you about scripts, tips, tricks and techniques to get past the gatekeepers and how to secure an appointment. I am going to tell you what to do to get that appointment simply and easily.

Tell the truth. That is it. It works for me and for everyone else who tries it. Just tell whomever you are calling the truth. Tell them who you are, your company name and why you are calling. Make sure the why part describes a benefit for the person you are calling, or at least shows them you are interested in helping them do something better, faster or cheaper.

When this person is willing to meet with you, schedule the appointment at a time that is mutually convenient. This might seem trite and obvious, but it is not done as often as it should be. When the appointment is mutually convenient, both of you are in the proper frame of mind. When one of you is pressed for time, or has other issues of concern, the presentation will not go as well as it should.

If you cannot schedule a mutually convenient time, go out of your way for the prospects. Never require the prospects to schedule the appointment at an inconvenient time for them. They will not be happy campers. Remember, the prospect has money you want for your products or services. Scheduling your appointments around their availability is not only good business, it is also a great first step in providing proactive customer service.

For retail store owners, the concept works the same way. Your appointment times are your hours of operation. Can you stay open later during the week, open on weekends, provide special appointment-only sales, or even make house calls? You will be pleasantly surprised with the growth in your business if you simply make yourself more available to prospects and customers.

Doing this gives you a double benefit. It is a great marketing tactic, which you can publicize. It also is a great customer service tactic, which you can teach your customers to publicize for you.

Step 4. Making the Presentation

This is your make or break time. Unless your marketing has been so terrific—and if you use the suggestions in this book they may very well be—you will have to make some type of presentation to get someone to buy what you are selling. There are many excellent books on how to make a sales presentation and others on how to make a presentation in general. Your goal at this point is to make enough of an impression on the prospect so he or she buys from you.

There is more that goes into the presentation than just showing your wares. How you look, how your store looks, how your presentation materials look, how you speak, how you answer questions, and how much you get the prospect involved with your presentation all have a decided effect on your final sale. Make sure that everything is as you would want it to be if someone were coming to sell to you; then try to make it slightly better. There have been several occasions where I have gained a client simply because they liked the way I looked and presented myself, rather than my presentation. And they told me so.

Begin your presentation with either a benefit statement or something of interest to the prospect. If you are in retail, never walk over to someone who comes into your store and say "Can I help you?" They invariably answer no, or say they are just looking. Go over to them, introduce yourself and say "How may I help you?" or "How long have you been considering purchasing an item like that?"

Now you have given them a chance to open up and say a few more words than no.

Never be pushy. Give prospects a chance to think and form their own opinions about what you are presenting. You can guide them, but do not force your ideas on them. In service presentations, it is a good idea to stop every few minutes and ask the prospect—or customer if this presentation is for additional business—his or her thoughts on what you have presented so far. To keep them interested, you need to break up the presentation and keep them involved.

Step 5. Handling Objections

There will be times during your presentation that prospects will have objections to what you are saying. Objections are nothing more than requests for more information. When someone tells you your price is too high, or they have to confer with someone else, or they are not interested right now, they are merely telling you that they do not have enough information to make an informed decision that they can live with.

Successful salespeople welcome, even thrive on objections. Think about it. Since an objection is nothing more than a request for more information, the prospect is telling you exactly how to tailor your presentation from that point on. If they say your price is too high (and by the way, if you have presented properly, price will not be an issue), you have to ask them "compared to what?" and then go on to build even greater perceived value so they think the price is fair.

If they tell you they have to speak to someone else about the decision, ask them who that person is and what you can do to provide the information directly to that person. Remember, they are only giving you another opportunity to customize your presentation and sell them your products or services.

You will encounter many more objections. However, only four or five will probably come up regularly. If this is the case, you need to revise your presentation to cover these objections before they surface. Also, the best way you can handle objections is to ask more questions.

For example, whenever you encounter an objection, ask the prospect or customer, "Aside from this objection, is there anything else that is preventing you from buying?" Or, "What else would I have to tell you to make you feel comfortable with this purchase?"

As a matter of fact, if you ask questions during your entire presentation, and listen carefully to the answers, the prospects will tell you exactly what you must do to sell to them.

Step 6. Closing the Sale

By this time, closing the sale is easy. I know there are books that tell you what to say and how to say it and at what time to make the close. Actually, you do not need any of these scripts to close a sale. If your presentation was done well, and you answered all the prospect's questions, the sale will close itself.

In fact, the number one reason salespeople fail is because they do not ask for the check or the order. Can you believe it? They go through the entire process, make the presentation and handle all the objections, and then hope the prospect says

"Where do I sign?" You have to ask them for the order or the check. You cannot be shy about it.

In retail, you just ask them if you can wrap it up for them. Ask them if that will be cash, check or charge. Ask them if there is anything else they would like to purchase today.

Whatever you do, ask for the order or tell the prospect what he or she must do next to confirm the sale. Sign the agreement. Initial the purchase order. Step over to the cash register. Ask for the money that will signify you have closed the sale. Anything.

Why is this the number one reason for sales failure? It is because people do not want to be rejected. If you do not ask for the order, they cannot say no. Then, you will not feel rejected.

If you do not ask for the order or the money, you may never get it. So, to close the sale, ask for it.

Step 7. Servicing Your Customers

Congratulations. You have made the sale and turned the prospect into your customer. Now, the marriage truly begins. You must provide superior customer service to your new customers, otherwise they will take their business to your competitors.

Here is where retailers can take a lesson from service providers. Service providers keep records of all their customers (sales), perhaps using a contact management or database program. They send out letters, newsletters, information and anything else they can think of that will help the customer, and will remind the customer they are constantly thinking of them.

Many retailers, on the other hand, take the cash at the register and never do anything to make the customer come back. Here are a few service suggestions that are also great marketing tools. The end result is that your future sales will be easier.

Collect the names and addresses of each customer. Do whatever you must do to capture their vital information. You can have them fill out an information sheet at the register so that you can send them fliers on special sales. Have them drop their business cards or a registration form into a contest leads box. Ask them to fill out a brief customer survey card before they leave; make sure their names and addresses are on the cards.

Then, you can consistently go back and mail them information or call them about special sales or programs just for them. While you use this as a marketing tactic, the customers will perceive your actions as excellent customer service. The end result is that they will buy more from you, and refer more people to you.

And, you already know that selling from referrals is the easiest sale of all, next to reselling a satisfied customer.

Basic Selling: A Summary

These are the seven basic steps you must take to be successful at sales. You can improve your skills with practice, by constant repetition, through reading, attending seminars, and trying these suggestions out in the real world. Every one of the seven steps can be made easier by effective marketing.

One of your sales goals should be to get the majority of your business to come from referrals. This makes your prospecting and qualifying steps much easier, or possibly unnecessary. Since the prospect is positively receptive, your appointment scheduling and presentation are also easier. There will probably be fewer objections and the close will take care of itself. Then, the ball is in your court to provide superior customer service, to make future marketing and selling even easier.

For some added help in improving your sales skills, read the charts in the Appendix. They include information on a standard sales presentation, how to set up a basic sales plan, 10 steps to successful selling, how to handle objections, how to close a sale, and information on how to improve your telemarketing (teleselling) skills.

Your Turn

► List the activities you conduct in each of the seven steps of selling.

- Prospecting
- Qualifying
- Scheduling Appointments
- Making Presentations
- Handling Objections
- Closing
- Servicing the Customer

► Which areas are you strong in? Which areas need improvement?

► List the things you will do to improve your selling skills.

► List the activities, techniques or things you do to attract a prospect's **a**ttention, to get them **i**nterested in what you are selling, to increase their **d**esire to buy from you, and then get them to **a**ct on making a purchase. (See Appendix for AIDA formula.)

THE NEXT LEVEL OF SELLING

You now have the basics of selling in your repertoire of skills. Unfortunately, not every sales situation or prospect/customer encounter lends itself to one of the seven steps of selling. No one person or event is always easily categorized. For example, retailers may never prospect or qualify someone, whereas financial planners or stock brokers should always qualify a potential customer. The seven steps of selling work well for the latter group of small business persons, but not for the former, all the time.

Therefore, you need some additional skills that can take you beyond the traditional selling arena. These skills, which I call Extraordinary Selling Power™, teach you how to communicate more effectively with prospects and customers, how to listen to their verbal and nonverbal communications and how to literally speak their language.

Have you ever had a situation where you thought the sale was made and for no conscious, apparent reason, the person did not buy from you? No matter how you tried, you could not figure out what caused you to lose the sale?

At some point, you and the customer or prospect very likely began speaking different languages. Think about it. When you are uncomfortable speaking with someone it is because they are using words that do not fit your communication style. Go into an auto dealership and tell the salesperson you like the way a certain car looks. If that person starts talking to you about the quiet ride, the hum of the engine, and the vacuum "pop" the door makes when it closes, you will definitely feel uncomfortable and not buy from that salesperson.

The techniques of Extraordinary Selling Power™ (ESP) help you overcome these potential problems. You actually become capable of "reading" people's minds. Add these skills to your basic selling skills and you will see your sales, closing ratio and income skyrocket.

ESP Starts with Knowing People

Remember how prospecting requires you to start by seeking out the best potential candidates to buy from you, and then qualifying them. People tend to sell better to other people who behave like themselves. The reason is simply that you are more comfortable with people who are like you. In selling, and in life, like attracts like, and opposites repel.

In one of my ESP training programs, a real estate agent told me she was having trouble selling to people who were very outgoing and expressive. She had no trouble selling people who like a lot of detail about what they were buying. She also said she thoroughly loved to tell people about every little detail of their purchase. For some reason, though, about three-fourths of her prospects went elsewhere. The solution was very easy.

People's behavior, or personality styles, can be categorized into four types: *Dominant* (or Driver), *Expressive, Solid* (or Amiable or Friendly) and *Analytical* (or Compliant or Cautious). Each behavioral type has specific characteristics associated with it.

Dominant people tend to be competitive, time intense, impatient, always seeking control, and they enjoy taking risks. They also tend either to interrupt you when you speak or to finish your sentences for you.

Expressive people like recognition, they are very sociable and they enjoy being the center of attention. They also tend to gesture a great deal when they communicate with you.

Dominant and Expressive types also tend to be assertive, with Dominants preferring to focus on tasks that must be completed and Expressives preferring to focus on people.

Solids are called that because they are stable, mature, good listeners and very friendly. Solids have some difficulty making decisions, especially when they think their decision can hurt someone's feelings. So, if you are ever going to lunch with three or four Solids, do not let them decide where to eat. If you do, they will change their minds so often so as not to hurt each other's feelings that you will starve.

Analyticals analyze everything. They love details, procedures, doing things the way things have always been done. They are very cautious about taking risks or getting involved with anything that requires changes.

Solids and Analyticals tend to be less assertive than their other two counterparts, while Analyticals focus on tasks and Solids focus on people.

The charts that follow give you more detail on the characteristics of each type of behavioral style. Now, how do you sell to each style?

Interpersonal Styles Matrix

High Responsiveness
Open
Relationship-Oriented
Wants to be Liked

SOLID

EXPRESSIVE

Low Assertiveness
Slow-Paced
Indirect
Avoids Risk

High Assertiveness
Fast-Paced
Direct
Results-Oriented

ANALYTICAL

DOMINANT

Low Responsiveness
Self-Contained
Task-Oriented
Disciplined

Interpersonal Styles: Personality Factors

SOLID

- [ ] Needs People
- [ ] Listener
- [ ] Status Quo
- [ ] No Risks
- [ ] No Pressure
- [ ] Counselor/Help Others
- [ ] Questioning
- [ ] Insecure/Needs Reassurance
- [ ] Supportive
- [ ] No Goals
- [ ] No Conflict
- [ ] Soft-Hearted

EXPRESSIVE

- [ ] Dreamer
- [ ] Unrealistic Goals
- [ ] Creative; Ideas Flow
- [ ] Flighty
- [ ] Needs Approval/Compliments
- [ ] Generalizes
- [ ] Persuasive, Outgoing
- [ ] Opinionated
- [ ] Fast Decisions
- [ ] Excitable
- [ ] Enthusiastic, Shows Confidence

ANALYTICAL

- [ ] Planner
- [ ] Details
- [ ] Slow Decisions
- [ ] Technical
- [ ] Must Be Right
- [ ] Conservative/Cautious
- [ ] Organizer
- [ ] Low Pressure
- [ ] Logical
- [ ] Precise/Critical
- [ ] Problem Solver
- [ ] Persistent
- [ ] Follows Procedures
- [ ] Neat and Organized

DOMINANT

- [ ] Goal-Oriented/Results-Oriented
- [ ] Impatient
- [ ] Task-Oriented/High Achiever
- [ ] Workaholic
- [ ] Decisive
- [ ] Time Effective
- [ ] Blunt
- [ ] Administrative
- [ ] Opinionated/Stubborn
- [ ] Innovative
- [ ] Tough/Firm in Relationships
- [ ] Control-Oriented
- [ ] Competitive/Loves Challenge

Behavioral Style: Goals and Motives

Behavioral Style	Their Goal	Their Fear	Their Basis for Buying	General Strategy for Selling to Them
D	Personal Control	Being Taken Advantage Of	**What** Product/Service Does for Them	The Potential Results of the Product/Service
E	Social Influence	Social Rejection	**Who** Is Using Your Product/Service (And What They Say about It)	The Product/Service "Appeal to People"
S	Stable Relationships	Loss of Stability	**How** Your Product/Service Will Help Stabilize Conditions for Them	The "Support Provided" by This Product/Service
A	Accuracy	Criticism of Their Efforts	**Why** Your Product/Service Is a Logical Investment for Them	The "Track Record" of the Product/Service How Has the Product/Service Performed in the Past

Interpersonal Style

FAST TRACK STYLE INDICATOR

Ask the first question below, then follow the arrow to determine the person's behavioral tendencies and interpersonal style.

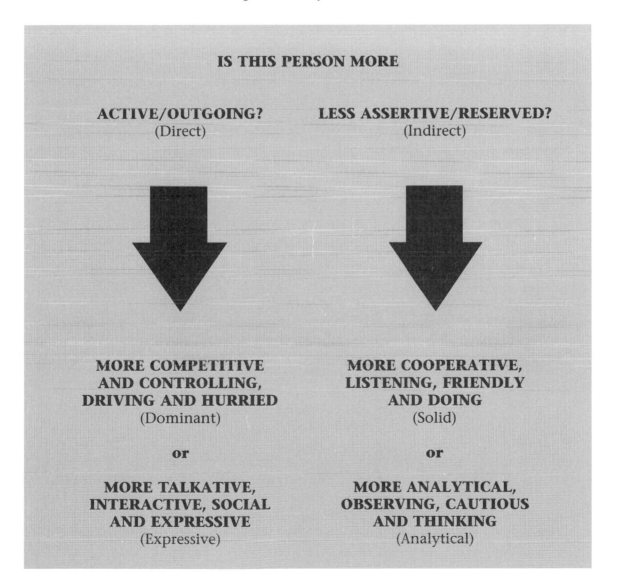

IS THIS PERSON MORE

ACTIVE/OUTGOING?
(Direct)

LESS ASSERTIVE/RESERVED?
(Indirect)

MORE COMPETITIVE AND CONTROLLING, DRIVING AND HURRIED
(Dominant)

MORE COOPERATIVE, LISTENING, FRIENDLY AND DOING
(Solid)

or

or

MORE TALKATIVE, INTERACTIVE, SOCIAL AND EXPRESSIVE
(Expressive)

MORE ANALYTICAL, OBSERVING, CAUTIOUS AND THINKING
(Analytical)

Selling to a Dominant

When you sell to a dominant, there is no time for socializing. Get right to the point. Show the dominant prospect how *what* you are selling will increase their bottom line or their prestige. Tell them how it will help them achieve their goal sooner. Give them only the most pertinent facts and save the details for someone else. Always allow them to feel in control of the sales situation. If you have trouble closing the dominant prospect, present them with a challenge. Dominants love challenges, and this one action on your part may get them to close themselves.

Selling to an Expressive

Expressives love to be flattered. Ask them questions about themselves and let them tell you how great they are. Marvel at their accomplishments. Allow them to be enthusiastic. Never do or say anything that would hurt or test the expressive's ego. They crave social recognition. They also love to show how confident and good they are at something. Give them opportunities to do this. Tell them who else is using what you are selling. They will then silently compare how they will get more benefits out of using your product or service than the name you just dropped. When they reach a decision, they will close themselves.

Selling to a Solid

Solids are the friendly type, so be friendly. With this prospect, you want to spend time in social conversation. Solids need to get to know you and to feel comfortable with you, to buy from you. If they like you, they will listen intently to your entire presentation. When they ask questions, give answers and then reassure them that the question was a good one and that your product or service will only improve what they already have or make a situation more stable. Solids are afraid of rapid change and too much conflict. A hard sell approach here usually does not work. Also, inform the solid of the support and service you will provide after the sale. This will increase their comfort zone with you and what you are selling.

Selling to an Analytical

These are your detail-oriented people. They love facts and figures, so give them what they want. Tell them why they should buy your product, support your statement with appropriate facts, and then tell them again. Make sure you have all your facts straight, because they will check on you. Also, analyticals are conservative and they like to follow rules and procedures. Your sales approach with them should do the same. Make sure your presentation focuses on the logic of the buy, not the emotion. This is true even though most people buy on emotion and justify on logic. Analyticals do their very best to keep their emotions out of buying/selling situations.

You now have the first part of the Extraordinary Selling Power™ equation. You must know how people behave and react to other people's—your—behavior before you can successfully sell them anything. Some people know these things instinctively, but the nice thing is that you can learn how to recognize people's behavioral styles. Review the charts and pick out two or three characteristics for each style, study them and learn to recognize them when they occur.

If you do nothing else but recognize and adapt to a prospect's behavioral style, you will see your sales increase dramatically.

The Importance of Listening

To communicate effectively, you need a speaker and a listener. Although making your presentation is important to your success as a salesperson, developing your listening skills are more important if you want to become an Extraordinary Sales Person. So, when your prospects or customers talk, you listen.

When you listen, let them know you are listening. Give them feedback. Nod your head, open your eyes wider, say "uh huh, I see, go on," or something of that nature to tell the speaker you are paying close attention. If you misunderstood something they said, ask them to repeat it. Then repeat it back to them to make sure you both are clear on the meaning of what was said.

After all, effective communication is only effective when the listener gets the same message the speaker intended for him or her to get. And you let each other know this through feedback.

Here are several other ways to help you communicate more effectively and develop your Extraordinary Selling Power™.

Build Rapport

People like doing business with people they like. And people like people who are like them. How do you get people to perceive you are like them? You build rapport.

Have you ever met someone and got along with them instantly? The rapport was immediate.

What caused that rapport? Was it the way the person looked, stood, sat or spoke? Was it their similar accent, background, experiences or lifestyle? You get the picture. When people are more like you, you tend to like them more. And they will like you more. The result, in a selling situation, is that they will buy more from you, more often.

In Extraordinary Selling Power™ training programs, I teach two very powerful ways to build rapport. There are also variations of these basic techniques, which you can learn and apply.

Pacing

Pacing is simply playing follow the leader. You pace what the other person is doing: You follow their lead. You stand or sit using the same posture. You speak at the same rate of speed. You try to breathe the same way they are. You move as quickly or as slowly as they do. You use similar gestures.

Pacing is probably not a new concept to you. You do it all the time, although you may not have had a label for your behavior. You pace naturally when you are walking and talking with someone. Your goal with pacing is to try to establish a subconscious rapport with the other person, so both of you perceive the similarities you possess. This keeps everything positive and focuses on strengths in a relationship, rather than focusing on differences—which could undermine the selling relationship.

Here are some other things you can pace: eye blink rate, breathing depth and rate, frequency of taking a drink if you are having a meal together, ordering similar meals in a restautant, vocabulary, voice volume, head tilt—the list goes on. Also, remember to pace the behavioral style characteristics of the person with whom you are communicating. Check the charts on the previous pages to remind you who speaks and moves fast, who is assertive, who likes details and who wants to be friendly.

When you pace someone correctly, you develop the *rhythm of rapport*. Once you develop this rhythm, your closing ratio will increase, and your prospects will become a repeat customer because they not only likes doing business with you, they like you as a person.

Modeling, Mirroring and Matching

This three-M approach to rapport building takes pacing to a higher level. When you pace someone, you have to be careful not to make it so obtrusive and obvious that it becomes offensive. Use one of these three techniques to help build and solidify your rapport, without turning the prospect or customer off.

Modeling is a technique that you probably learned and used in childhood. This is how you learned to walk and talk. You watched what the big people were doing, listened to what they said and copied them. Modeling is basically copying the behavior or actions of someone else: a role model.

Copying behavior applies to mirroring and matching as well. Modeling someone means doing something similar to what they are doing. You copy their behavior without being offensive or a nuisance. The key to making any of these three techniques work is to wait about two seconds before you copy the behavior. This brief time lag will make your actions seem more natural to the prospect.

While modeling a behavior is copying it by doing something similar, *mirroring* a behavior is copying it by doing the mirror-image opposite. If your prospect lifts one hand to make a point, you lift the opposite hand after an appropriate delay. If your prospect crosses his or her right foot over the left, you wait a couple of seconds and cross your left foot over your right. Respond as if you were an image in the mirror.

The last of the three-M approaches is matching. This is where you have to be the most careful. *Matching* means doing exactly what the prospect is doing. The key here is to wait the two or three seconds, and move slowly. You never want the other person to think you are mimicking them. Matching another person's body movements and body language is a very powerful rapport builder. It strengthens the perception that you and the prospect are alike in many ways, and that he or she should do business with you.

This is the second set of skills you need to have Extraordinary Selling Power™. Combine pacing and three-M techniques with your knowledge of behavioral styles and you are well on your way to becoming an Extraordinary Sales Person. Use these modeling, mirroring and matching techniques when you speak with a prospect or customer. Model, mirror or match the words they use to describe their situations. When you do this, you develop a subconscious link to their sensory perceptual communication style, also known as their representational style.

When you communicate in their language, you enter their world and model of reality, and your selling becomes much easier. Prospects begin to close themselves. They cannot wait to buy from you again and again. Plus, your intimate knowledge of their preferred behavioral styles and your ability to build rapport make all your communications that much more effective.

You are now ready for the third and final part of the Extraordinary Selling Power™ equation. You need to learn to speak your prospects' language, as well as to communicate in the language they use to perceive events. This may sound ethereal, but it is really quite simple. What you say and how you say it are most important when you communicate.

In selling, as with any type of interpersonal communication, perception is everything. Here is how you help prospects and customers perceive your message exactly as you intended it to be.

Three Ways We Communicate

All communication is some combination of visual, vocal and verbal. Visual relates to what we do, our body language and nonverbal behavior. Vocal is how we sound to other people, such as the pitch of our voices, our rate of speech and our tone. Verbal refers to the words we use.

The most remarkable thing about these three ways of communicating is that the most common way, verbally, is the least important. When we communicate, or try to sell somebody something, what is said accounts for only 7% of the entire message. How we sound (vocal) accounts for 38% of the message we are trying to get across, and what we look like and how we behave or move around (nonverbal behavior) takes up the other 55% of the message's meaning.The graph on the next page illustrates these percentages.

What this means to you is that to be a successful salesperson, use words that your prospects and customers understand, and motivate them to buy with your positive and self-confident tone of voice, rate of speech and behavior.

Here is an example to help you understand this better. Have you ever walked into a store to buy something, known what you wanted and gotten turned off when the salesperson came over and began explaining things to you? You fully understood the meaning of the words, but you did not jell on the level of vocal and/or visual communication. It may have been because the words and the tone and the behavior were not in line, or congruent. For communication to be successful, it must be congruent.

Here is another example. What if you were trying to sell somebody your product or service, and you said you were very enthusiastic about what the product could do for the prospect? However, you said it in a very slow, bored tone of voice. Do you think the prospect would become enthusiastic and buy what you are selling? Hardly, because your words, tone and actions were not congruent.

How We Communicate

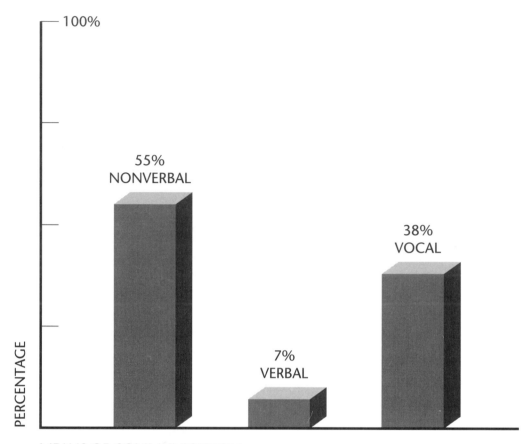

100%

55%
NONVERBAL

38%
VOCAL

7%
VERBAL

PERCENTAGE

MEANS OF COMMUNICATION

Communication Modes

We communicate verbally in one of three primary modes: visual, auditory or kinesthetic. We are most comfortable saying and hearing words that create pictures (visual), relate to sounds (auditory), or access our feelings (kinesthetic). When we meet someone who uses words we are comfortable with, we communicate very well. We establish an instant and subconscious rapport.

Let us say you get everything together but you still cannot seem to make the sale. It is because the words you are using are not the same words that the prospect or customer is comfortable in hearing. Think about this and you will see (hear, feel) it makes more sense.

When we communicate with someone who does not use the words and phrases we are comfortable with, we begin to feel uneasy. We tune them out and stop listening. To be comfortable with a prospect, or anyone, and to communicate effectively and successfully, you must use the words of their language.

Selling to a Visual

Visuals are easy to see in any situation. They stand tall, keep their heads erect, breathe shallow and rapidly and speak fast. The reason they speak fast is because they are talking based on the movies in their head. Therefore, their words must keep up with the pictures going through their minds.

Visuals also gesture with their hands up around their face or their eyes. They will point to their eyes and say, "I see what you are saying." They can also break off a conversation in midsentence, start a conversation on a completely different topic, break that off and pick up the original conversation in the middle of the original sentence. They are able to do this because the movies in their minds have begun to rerun.

Visuals also tend to look up a great deal to help them picture what they want to say.

To sell to these types of people, use words that create pictures. Help them see what you are selling. Get them to visualize how they will use and benefit from your product or service. Illustrate for them how successful they will be. If you have a presentation book or slide show, use it.

Selling to an Auditory

Auditories love the sound of their own voices. In fact, they love sounds in general. They like to hear crisp, distinct sounds, especially when someone speaks to them. Auditories hate to have someone cut off the ends of their words or slur their speech.

Auditories speak slightly slower than visuals. Auditories point to their ears to hear what you are saying. They like to be told things. When you explain something to an auditory, they will tell you they understand by using a phrase such as "That rings true for me," or "That's clear as a bell to me."

Auditories breathe from the middle of their chests, so their breathing rate is somewhat slower and deeper than visuals. Auditories use gestures around the chest area and keep their palms up, so they can point to their ears, if need be.

To sell to an auditory, describe the sound of success when using your products or services. Tell them how others will talk about their great purchase. Create a symphony for their ears, and they will buy from you forever.

Selling to a Kinesthetic

Kinesthetics are the feelers of the world. They like to touch things, to sense things and to learn about the world through their feelings. Most young children are kinesthetics. That is why they touch everything, wherever they go. Kinesthetics are also the slowest moving of the three types of communicators, because they have to get a feel for everything they are told or see.

Kinesthetics breathe very deeply, and process information "in their gut" to get a true feeling for what is going on. They speak more slowly than the other two types of people, and they gesture around their midsection. Again, they are trying to get a feel for everything.

To sell to a kinesthetic, help them feel what you are selling them. Give them a sense of how they will be successful. If you sell a product, let them try it out first. Get them physically involved with what you are selling. Develop your presentation to bring the kinesthetic into it.

The Number One Reason People Do Not Sell Well

Have you figured it out yet? It is really quite simple. The number one reason people do not sell well is because they are communicating in a different perceptual/representational style than the prospect or customer is perceiving them in. More practically, if I am trying to sell you my marketing consulting services, and I show you how to see the benefits of my service, I illustrate what you will get from working with me, and I paint a picture of your successful business in the future, I may be way off base in my presentation if you prefer to hear about the sounds of success or you need to get a feel for what I am talking about.

Test it out next time you speak with someone or try to sell someone something. Listen for the words, mostly verbs, they use. To help you identify the styles more correctly, review the charts on perceptual analysis in Appendix IV until you become familiar with the most common words used by each style. Once you have identified their style, build rapport by using their preferred words back to them. When they hear you speaking their language, they will open up and become more relaxed with you. The chances for you to make a sale now are much greater.

Four ESP Questions to Lead You to Sales Success

One of the things every sales training course teaches you is to ask questions. They teach you the difference between open- and closed ended questions, and how each type helps you control the conversation and bring the sale to a close.

These types of questions are effective and you should know about them. Ask open-ended questions when you are seeking more information. Ask closed-ended questions when you want to guide a prospect or customer along a specific train of thought or towards your close.

Here are four specific questions you can adapt to your business or industry that will get the prospect or customer to tell you exactly how to sell them. When you can use these questions automatically, you will have come a long way in developing your Extraordinary Selling Power™.

1. What has been your previous experience with someone else selling you a product or service similar to mine? The prospect will tell you about the good, bad or ugly, or the fact that there was never a previous purchase. If they had a good or bad experience, they will use very descriptive words to describe it to you. Listen carefully to the words and watch their nonverbal behavior. If they never bought anything like you are selling, ask the prospect to describe a purchase he or she was happy with. Then listen and watch for the same things.

What you will get from this exchange are the elements of the buying experience that the prospect likes or dislikes, and you can play it back to him or her to develop rapport.

2. How did you go about making your decision to buy that product or service? Again, watch and listen carefully. The descriptive words will reveal the way the prospect perceives things. The answer to this question will also give you the prospect's buying strategy. For example, the prospect may tell you he or she looked at many competitive products (visual), discussed it with colleagues in other companies (auditory) and then tried out the product to get a feel for it (kinesthetic).

You now know the prospect buys based on a visual, auditory, kinesthetic strategy and all you have to do is paint pictures first, tell him or her things second and give him or her a chance to get a feel for what you are selling. Knowing the prospect's buying strategy is an extremely powerful selling skill.

3. What benefits or outcomes do you want from my product or service? They may have already told you the answer to this question during their discussion of questions 1 or 2 above. However, you need to ask this one specifically to get them to guide you in customizing your presentation. Once you know what they are seeking as benefits, you can tailor your presentation to emphasize those benefits. Of course, you must still communicate in their preferred style: visual, auditory or kinesthetic.

4. What specific questions do you need me to answer now, before we continue? Their answer will provide you with their buying criteria, what they value, like and dislike, and their concerns when making a purchase. Their answers will bring out many objections up front, so you can answer them in your presentation.

These four questions will help you improve your Extraordinary Selling Power™. You can use them exactly as they are, or you can customize them for your own needs. The key is to use the questions so the prospect reveals buying strategies, communication strategies and purchasing preferences. Then, tailor your sales presentation to those answers.

One other thing you must do to become a successful sales professional—develop your listening skills. The best salespeople in the world are also the best listeners. They listen very carefully to what is being said, which lets customers and prospects sell themselves. Successful salespeople listen with their ears, their eyes and their minds, since messages are sent in a variety of ways. They also get actively involved with the conversation and provide feedback to the prospect to let him or her know they are being listened to.

You can train yourself to listen to the prospect or customer's message by watching his or her eyes. Eye movement tells you a great deal about what the person is thinking, and how he or she processes information. For example, people who look up before speaking to you are picturing something in their minds. When they look to either side, they are listening to a conversation in their mind. And, when they look down to the right, they are getting a feel for what they are saying or what you just said.

These basic tips on watching eye movements can help you become more successful when you sell. Of course, more training and practice is required. You can definitely become well versed in these techniques. When you do, watch your sales soar.

How I Stay Successful

It is difficult to always be up when you constantly have to sell yourself or your business's product or service. Aside from keeping a positive mental attitude and conditioning myself psychologically for success on a daily basis, I rely on a few other tools to help me. These productivity and planning tools have enabled me to grow my business by keeping me on track toward my goals and on time with my clients.

Planning for productivity and success is crucial to achieving both. You have to know what you want to achieve by when, and who can help you do it. You need some sort of planning system for yourself, which also keeps you informed about your prospects and customers. Every successful salesperson and marketer I know has some type of system they use to keep them informed, on track and ahead of the game. You have to find the one that is right for you. Here are some suggestions on software programs and paper planning systems that I have found successful.

For tracking prospects and customers, and even for keeping records of their appointments, I recommend two software programs. Both ACT! from Contact Software International (1840 Hutton #200, Carrollton, Texas 75006, 214-919-9500) and Commence™ from Jenson-Jones, Inc. (Parkway 109 Office Center, 328 Newman Springs Rd., Red Bank, NJ 07701, 800-289-1548) will help manage your contacts and correspondence, along with keeping you straight on your appointments.

If you prefer paper and pen, look into systems from Day-Timers (One Day-Timer Plaza, Allentown, PA 18195-215-266-9000) or Franklin Institute (PO Box 25127, Salt Lake City, Utah, 84125, 800-654-1776). Keith Clark (101 O'Neil Rd., Sidney, NY 13838, 607-543-9411) also offers a planner system.

I have used all these systems at one time or another and find them very effective. Each of these systems can be customized to suit your needs. They all even contain contact management pages to track your meetings and calls with prospects and customers. Franklin Institute has a computer program called Ascend that works seamlessly with their planner. Keith Clark has a software program called At-A-Glance Time Management, designed to work with their planner. Both of these also keep track of prospects and clients.

The first step is to determine which planning system you want to use: computerized, paper or both, as I do. The reason I use both types is that I do not take my desktop computer with me on sales or client calls. I rely on the paper system to schedule my appointments, take my notes, and write my To Do's, which I then transfer to my database. You can do the same. Whatever approach you use, customize the system so it works the way you do. Finally, follow these five steps to planning for productivity and success:

1. Plan your next day's activities the night before, giving yourself 15–30 minutes of quiet planning time.

2. Review your daily plan in the morning before you get started.

3. Set long-term, short-term and daily task goals to guide you toward success.

4. Track your efforts. Keep notes of what you do, who you do it with and what happens.

5. Evaluate your efforts in terms of their contributions toward your goals and make revisions, when and where necessary, as you plan for the next day.

Follow these five steps and you will see an increase in your productivity, along with a natural improvement in your sales success.

Salespeople as Negotiators

A word about the art and skill of negotiation—every situation or personal contact, especially a selling situation, is a negotiation of some sort. Even in everyday interpersonal communications, we are usually trying to convince someone to accept our message, align with our position, change their mind or buy our product.

To learn about negotiation skills, you can read any of the hundreds of books published on the subject or attend a seminar. You can also look into a software program called Negotiator Pro™ by Beacon Expert Systems (35 Gardner Rd., Brookline, MA 02146, 800-448-3308). This program can be very helpful in improving your ability to negotiate and close sales.

Very simply, the program determines your behavioral and negotiating styles, as well as that of the person you are going to negotiate with. It then asks your responses to a series of questions and recommends a course of action for you to take during your negotiation. A textbook on negotiation skills is included with the program. Add these skills to your selling repertoire and you will become more successful than you ever dreamed.

Tying It All Together

There you have it. Try one of the systems or programs I recommend, or create your own. The important thing is that you do something in these areas to keep you moving in the right direction.

Now, practice your new found skills. Combine the behavioral style of prospects with their communication style; mirror, match or model it back to them to develop rapport. You will see your sales soar. Here are a few examples.

A stock broker took my course and earned 50% more than the company's average income for a first-year account executive. An insurance agent doubled his income in six months after completing the seminar and using the techniques. A real estate agent who had not made a sale in four months finished the course, went out and listed six properties, and then sold three of them within three months.

And I have been very fortunate. Using all these ESP techniques, I made 18 major sales presentations in 1992 and closed 16 of them. That is not a bad closing percentage for anyone in any industry.

These same skills and techniques work in retail. Plus, you can use the Extraordinary Selling Power™ techniques to provide superior customer service. That is because sales and service are two sides of the same coin; they both depend totally on effective communication.

ASK YOURSELF

▶ Describe your preferred communication style: visual, auditory or kinesthetic.

▶ Discuss the types of prospects or customers you feel most comfortable with. Who do you sell more to?

▶ Compare your verbal presentation with your tone of voice and nonverbal behavior. Is everything congruent?

▶ Describe what would happen if a dominant, visual person tried to sell your product or service to a kinesthetic, analytical person?

▶ What type of planning and productivity system do you use? How well does it work for you in keeping you on track and on time, plus keeping a record of your contacts?

▶ Select someone in your life with whom you get along extremely well. What are your common grounds? Do you "speak the same language"? Do you like the same things? Now, choose someone you dislike and answer the same questions. What prevents you from developing a rapport with this person?

COMMON-SENSE CUSTOMER SERVICE AND BEYOND

PLAIN OLD COMMON SENSE

Customer service and service quality are the buzzwords for succeeding in business today. For your small business to attract and keep loyal customers, to make a profit to be successful, you must provide customer service that is far superior to that provided by your competitors.

A great deal has been written about customer service and how businesses should treat their customers. Despite all the writings on the topics, much of customer service comes down to plain old common sense. Simply put, customer service involves everything you and your employees do to satisfy customers. That means you give them what they want and make sure they leave happy. If you just manage complaints, offer refunds or exchanges on returns, and smile at customers, you only provide a small part of excellent customer service. Customer service also means going out of your way for the customer, doing everything possible to satisfy the customer and making decisions that benefit the customer—even at the expense of the business.

Now, do not believe for a minute that I am saying you should give away the store to the customer. I am saying you must know when and how often the customer is right. Make all your service decisions based on the situation, what the customer wants, and how it affects your business. Treat every customer and service situation as individual and unique. Do not let inflexible rules and regulations, policies and procedures stop you from making your customers happy. Just use good old common sense.

THE IMPORTANCE OF CUSTOMER SERVICE

How important is customer service to the success of your business? Many people believe that it can make or break you. Consider this. You and your competitors are selling the same product or service at basically the same price. You really have nothing within the product or service to differentiate yourselves from each other. This being the case, what makes customers buy from you instead of your competitors?

Could it be the way you and your employees treat them? How about how you answer the telephone, or listen to their requests for information on what you are selling? What about the appearance of your store or office? All these things relate to customer service and the impressions customers have of you. If these impressions and perceptions are positive, they probably will do business with you. If they are negative, or if you have done something to upset a customer, you can be sure he or she will go down the street to one of your competitors.

Think about the last time you had poor service, either at a restaurant, an airport, or a retail store, or even at a health club. Remember how you felt. Why would you want your customers to experience any of those negative or painful feelings? You know how you perceived the situation and what you planned to do about it. If you decided to take your business elsewhere, do you think your customers will do the same?

Using common sense to provide superior customer service simply means you and your staff must be nice to the customers. Treat them as you want to be treated. Even better, treat them as they want to be treated. Then, give them something extra to surprise them—something they did not expect.

The Payoff of Superior Customer Service

Several years ago, you could not pay some small businesses to train their employees to provide good customer service. Either the business did not view the training as important, or they did not think the employees warranted training beyond specific job skills. Or, they felt that customers would come in, buy, and leave, and it really did not matter if you were nice to them or not. While there was a time when people would just accept how you treated them and continue to do business with you, this is no longer true. People are more educated, more value conscious and demand more for their dollar. If you do not provide them with great customer service, they will find someone who will.

Customer service pays; it does not cost you anything. Yes, it may cost you up-front in training programs for your staff. And, it may cost you up-front in revamping or revising your service delivery systems. But, in the long run, it always pays off. The way it pays off the most is in long-term customer retention. Keeping customers and doing business with them repeatedly is much less expensive than trying to find new customers all the time.

Some small businesses know the cost of acquiring a new customer, while others do not have a clue what new customer acquisition costs them. The ones who know what it costs are bending over backwards to keep customers happy. Furthermore, many business owners are not even aware of the extraordinary costs of losing a customer. They just figure that if someone stops doing business with them one day, another person will begin. Wrong!

Here are three things you must know about the payoff for providing excellent customer service. First, it costs five to six times more to acquire a new customer than it does to do business with a current or former customer. So, if you were able to calculate the cost of acquiring a new customer, and let us say that it is $500, and you figure out that it costs you only about $100 to do business with an old customer, that is a $400 savings that becomes profit in your business.

Second, whenever you lose a customer, there are costs associated with replacing them, the loss of revenue their business would have provided during the replacement period. Add to this something we call lost opportunity revenue. This is all the potential money you could have made from the customer if you kept them loyal and they continued to purchase from you over an extended period of time.

The third thing is the cost of negative word-of-mouth. Whenever you lose customers, it is usually due to a bad experience they had with you. You can control 96%–99% of the reasons people stop doing business with you, depending on your type of business. So in reality, you should only lose a small number of customers. But, if you dissatisfy even one customer, that person may tell up to 20 people about the bad service they received. The odds are these 20 people will not do business with you at all. Calculate that lost opportunity revenue over a three-, five- or 10-year period.

Add the costs of these three reasons together and you get a pretty good idea of how valuable and profitable it is to provide superior customer service, or how very costly it would be if you provided poor service. (For more information on calculating the cost of poor customer service, see my books *Beyond Customer Service* and *Measuring Customer Satisfaction,* also by Crisp Publications.) With this in mind, the question to ask yourself is not whether you can afford to train your staff to provide excellent customer service. Rather, can you really afford *not* to? Compare the payoff in money earned or saved by keeping your customers against what it costs when you lose them.

To put it very simply, customer service and long-term customer retention and satisfaction are vitally important to your success in business.

Common-Sense Customer Service

High quality customer service is as much a marketing tool for your business as it is a management approach or philosophy. Service quality improves your marketing. It motivates customers to tell others about you, and these referrals essentially create a customer sales force. Remember, the least expensive way to acquire new customers is through word of mouth referrals and what better way to get new customers than having their friends tell them to do business with you.

Good service also improves and makes management easier because everybody is committed to satisfying the customer. Employees are happier knowing they can do whatever it takes, without fear of reprisal or repercussions, to satisfy the customer. This makes the customers happier. The results are increased productivity and profitability, simply because everyone is working toward the same goal: customer satisfaction and retention.

Now that you know that quality customer service is based on good common sense, here are some ideas for you to provide common-sense customer service. Later in this chapter, I will show you some service marketing techniques that take you beyond customer service.

SEVEN COMMON-SENSE CUSTOMER SERVICE IDEAS

1. **Develop a customer service system for your business.** This includes policies and procedures for handling customers in all situations. Make sure these policies and procedures are flexible, and even breakable, if need be.

2. **Keep the customer service system easily accessible and very easy for customers to use.** When people come to you for service, they should get help from a live person who is available when the customer needs them, not when the employee is ready. If you use a voice menu system on your telephone, keep the options to a minimum. Customers hate to wait—and wade—through a long description of menu choices.

3. **Be proactive in your customer service.** Try to provide service to people even before they do business with you. Be open earlier and stay open longer. Be available on weekends or in the evenings if that is what your customers need. Send everyone a thank-you note for buying from you. Give them a gift if they make a large purchase or many purchases from you. Call them and tell them you appreciate their business. Do something positive for your customers, as often as you can, before a competitor does. Believe me, it will not take much for a customer to switch loyalties, unless you make it difficult for them by providing outstanding customer service.

4. **Give everyone permission to serve.** When customers want service, they do not want to wait while an employee comes to you for permission to help them. Empower your people to serve customers immediately, on the spot, right away, without delay. Customers will appreciate this and show their appreciation with increased business.

5. **Give them reasons to write you testimonial letters, to brag about you, and to refer their family and friends—the ultimate compliment.** Go so far out of your way to service a customer that when you ask for a

testimonial letter—and you should ask as often as possible—that customer will be more than happy to oblige. Or, they will write you one without you asking for it.

6. **Do everything right the first time.** There really is no reason to make a mistake that affects the customer. If you do make a mistake, correct it and do it perfectly the second time. You do not get a third chance to make it up to a customer, unless you have provided such superior service in the past that the customer is willing to forgive your two mistakes. It happens, but it is rare. So, when you or your staff goof, give your customer something extra.

7. **Ask your customers what they expect from you and give them more than that.** Customer service is one thing, but keeping customers for life requires developing highly satisfied customers. And the way you satisfy a customer is to meet and exceed their expectations of you.

These seven common-sense customer service ideas have helped many small businesses increase their customer base and their profitability. Superior customer service makes marketing and selling easier, and these seven ideas will certainly help you in those areas. If you do nothing else but put these into play in your business, you should see a positive growth pattern developing. And, if you need some more ideas, here they are:

Seven More Ways to Service Your Customers

1. **Have a clear service vision, philosophy, mission and total management commitment.** The success of customer service programs in any company or small business is based on total management or ownership commitment. You, as the owner, president, or CEO, must develop and communicate a clear and concise service vision for your company. Your service vision and commitment to the customer should be verbalized as part of the company's service mission statement. Think about having it printed, framed and hung on a wall where your staff and customers can see it every day.

2. **Know your internal and external customers.** For your customer service programs to be successful, know your customers intimately and understand them totally. Find out what your buying customers like about you, your staff and your business in general; what they dislike, what they want you to change, how they want you to change it; what they need, want and expect from you, when they need it; what motivates them to buy from you, what motivates them to buy from your competitors; what satisfies them and what you must do to maintain their loyalty and retain them as customers over time. The most effective way to do this is simply to ask your customers to provide you with this information.

    When you start to know your customers, you must continue learning about them. Their needs and expectations change on a regular—even daily—basis. Keep up with them and their changing needs. Call them at least once a month. See them, either at their place of business or their homes. Find out how they are doing and what they need. Ask them to meet with you on an individual or small group basis to make recommendations to help you improve your service.

    Provide this same type of treatment to your internal customers, your employees. If you want your people to provide superior customer service, treat your staff accordingly. Give them the same courtesy and treatment you extend to buying customers.

3. **Measure your service quality performance.** What gets measured gets done. It is that simple. Even though customer service is apparently intangible, you can still measure it. You can still develop performance standards that are objective and specific to your business. These standards will subconsciously motivate your employees to improve their service to customers. You can increase that motivation by tying in an incentive for superior service, based on customer comments or ratings.

    These standards also serve as the basis for your customer satisfaction surveys. Ask your customers for their input on your service performance. They will be only too glad to tell you. And, if they criticize what you are doing, look at it as an opportunity to improve your business. After all, where else can you get all this great, free consulting advice?

4. **Good customer service begins with good people.** Good customer service and effective customer retention programs can only be provided by competent, qualified and well-trained people. Your service is only as good as the people who deliver it. If you want great customer service in your business, which starts with being nice to people, hire and train nice people.

Here is something you should think about. Customer service people tend to be the lowest-paid employees in an organization. They also suffer the fastest burnout. When you consider that customer service people have the first direct contact with your customers, this is really the opposite of what should be. Pay these people a higher salary than normal and work with them to keep them on the job. After compensation and training, give them the authority to make decisions that satisfy customers on the spot, even if they sometimes have to bend the company rules and regulations.

That is another hint for you that I am only too happy to repeat. Make sure your customer service rules, regulations, policies and procedures are flexible and your employees can bend them whenever they feel it is necessary. One of the worst things you can do while you try to provide great service is hide behind a policy or a rule. Customers do not care about your policies or rules. They only care about what you are going to do to satisfy them right now. Teach your people how to do this and let them do it. Your number of satisfied customers and referral-based new customers will increase.

5. **Reward service accomplishments.** Providing great customer service is not its own reward. Actually, in many small businesses, customer service is the least thankful job someone could have. Unfortunately, this is totally wrong, but it is true nonetheless. It is up to you to provide a more positive atmosphere, where your people can offer superior customer service.

One way to do this is always to reward and reinforce superior performance. Just as what gets measured gets done, what gets rewarded gets repeated. So, reward great service accomplishments in as many ways as you can. Provide your staff with financial and psychological rewards. Show them recognition for a job well done. Give out pins or stickers with JWD on them for that Job Well Done. You will be pleasantly surprised at how many people will proudly wear them.

And never, ever forget to recognize, praise and reward small wins and accomplishments, the same way you would applaud and dramatize major victories. Each major success is the result of many small successes along the way. Make sure your people know that, and make sure they know you know that.

Now that you have taken the time and made the effort to recognize and reward your staff, reward your customers for good customer behavior. When they buy from you over and over again, when they make a large individual purchase, when they refer new customers to you, when they help you run your business better, or when they just honor you by doing business with you, recognize and reward their efforts. They appreciate the recognition the same way your employees do.

How do you find out what your employees and customers consider as a valuable reward? You ask them.

6. **Keep in touch with your customers.** Maintain constant contact with your customers. Conduct continuous and ongoing research to learn from them. Ask them questions right after they buy, or do anything with your business that allows them to form an opinion. Send them surveys in the mail, run contests that require participation in a survey, hold focus groups to get perceptions and opinions of your business, call them on the telephone, develop a customer council to advise you on their needs and your service performance, take customers to lunch or dinner— do anything you must do to stay close to your customers.

Be aware that your relationship with your customer actually begins before the purchase is made. This is when you must activate your retention programs, and this is when the customer will get to see how much you really care. Arrange all customer interactions so they are win-win situations for both of you. The result will be more loyal customers and longer-term members.

7. **Work toward continuous improvement.** Even though you have designed easy-to-use, friendly, and easily accessible customer service systems, you have hired and trained the best staff possible, and you go out of your way to learn about and satisfy your customers' needs, you must remember that no system, business or program is perfect. Work continuously to improve your customer service programs and your retention activities.

Your attempts at continuous improvement will be viewed very positively by customers and employees. They will see this as your attempt to become even better than you already are. The results of continuously improving your customer service systems and programs are more satisfied customers, more business for you and your staff and greater profits.

These seven ideas will help you provide superior, common-sense customer service. They will also help you create an effective customer service system. Customer service pays, it does not cost. You must constantly work to provide the best service at all times. Your only goal for being in business is to satisfy your customers. Once this is done, growth, expansion and profits will take care of themselves. Follow these seven suggestions; you will find that it will be very easy for you to go beyond customer service to long-term customer retention.

Quality Customer Service: A Real-Life Example

This really happened to me and I am sure something similar has happened to you.

I was having lunch with two business associates in a very popular local restaurant. Since it was a late lunch, the restaurant was no longer crowded. In fact, servers were standing around waiting for customers.

We placed our orders and 30 minutes later, they had still not arrived. The server checked on them at our request and said they would be up shortly. Ten minutes later, we called the manager over and explained how long we were waiting for our food. He came back with our orders after another five minutes.

What do you think happened next? The food was cold and had to be sent back. Finally, after another 15 minutes—total time, so far was one hour—he returned with our hot lunches. To say the least, we were not happy.

The manager apologized profusely for the delay and for any problems. When it was time to pay for the meal, he picked up the check and again apologized, saying he hoped to see us back again soon.

His apologies and his taking care of delivering the food personally, as well as picking up the check, are all examples of great customer service. He did everything possible to right the wrongs. In the end, the only thing extra he should have done was provide each of us with a discount coupon that had to be redeemed by a certain date. This would have virtually assured him that we would be back and give his staff another chance to make it right.

Because of his efforts, you can be sure I, and my colleagues, will return and will not provide his restaurant with negative recommendations to our friends and associates. What he did is known as a *customer save*. He saved us from going to his competitors in the future.

Quality Customer Service: If Only It Could Happen This Way

This example is the ultimate in exceptional customer service. I saw it on a cartoon about a futuristic family who was traveling on vacation to a gambling resort. When they arrived, the hotel destroyed their car. Why? Because every guest gets a new car to go home in. Then, when they were ready to go up to their room and asked directions, the desk clerk said, "You don't go to your room. Your room comes to you." And sure enough, the room came down off of the building and landed in the lobby for the couple to enter.

Now, that is what I call room service.

How can you use these examples to improve your customer service? Think about it. I am sure you can come up with dozens of ways to serve your customers better.

If you need more convincing evidence about how important it is to provide superior customer service, read the "Startling Service Statistics" section in *Beyond Customer Service.* Here are the headlines for these 10 service statistics.

STARTLING SERVICE STATISTICS

1. Only 4% of customers ever complain.

2. For every complaint you receive, there are 26 other customers with unresolved complaints or problems, and six of those people have serious problems.

3. Between 54% and 70% of customers who complain to you will do business with you again if you resolve their complaint.

4. Dissatisfied customers tell 10–20 people about their dissatisfaction.

5. Satisfied customers tell three to five people about their positive experience.

6. It costs five to six times more to attract new customers than to keep old ones.

7. Businesses that provide superior customer service can charge more for their products and services, realize greater profits and increase their market share.

8. The lifetime value of a customer, or the amount of purchases that customer would make over a 10-year period, is worth more than the cost of returning to them the purchase price of one item.

9. Customer service is governed by the rules of 10s. If it costs $10,000 to get a new customer, it takes only 10 seconds to lose one, and 10 years to get over it or for the problem to finally be resolved.

10. Customers stop doing business with you because:

- 1% die
- 3% move away
- 5% seek alternatives or develop other business relationships
- 9% begin doing business with the competition
- 14% are dissatisfied with the product or service
- 68% are upset with the treatment they have received

You control 96%–99% of the reasons people stop doing business with you. And, since 68% think they have been treated poorly, you really have control over much more of the customer service situation than you may have thought possible.

What are you going to do so you do not become one of these startling service statistics?

Customers today are better educated than ever before. They are more careful about their purchases and the dollars they spend. They are tired of receiving poor service. They want value for their money, especially when they use discretionary income. They want good service and are willing to pay for it. Quite simply, customers expect more for their purchases; when you give it to them, they will pay for it. Through customer service and retention programs, you will be able to maintain your market share and competitive edge, keep your current customers, remain profitable and stay in business.

Ten Reasons for Poor Service

The thing that amazes me the most is that it is so easy to provide superior customer service. It is truly a matter of common sense. Yet, it seems so hard for many people to treat customers nicely.

People constantly complain about receiving poor customer service. Ask them why and you will probably receive a laundry list of reasons why companies give such poor service. Below are 10 of the more popular reasons for giving or receiving poor customer service. How many of them apply to your small business?

► No customer service philosophy within the company

► Poorly trained employees

► Uncaring employees

► Perceptual differences between what businesses think customers want and what customers actually want

► Perceptual differences between what business owners think they provide customers in the way of service, and what customers actually receive or perceive they receive

► Perceptual differences between the way small business owners think customers want to be treated and the way customers really want to be treated

► Employees are not empowered to provide good service, take responsibility and make decisions that will satisfy the customer

► Negative attitudes of employees toward customers— sometimes due to the negative attitudes of management toward its employees or how poorly management treats its employees

► Poor or improper handling and resolution of complaints

► No service standards, reward and recognition programs

You can probably add your own reasons to this list of 10. After you do, then do one more thing. Develop a system for measuring your customer service and levels of customer satisfaction. If you need help, read *Measuring Customer Satisfaction* (Crisp Publications, 1993) to learn how to do this. The information you get from these surveys will help you realize why it is imperative to not only provide superior customer service, but to go beyond customer service and do everything in your power to acquire, maintain and retain loyal customers and members.

Before moving on to how you retain customers, one more point must be made about customer loyalty. People are loyal to you because they feel they are treated well, they receive good value for their money and they are psychologically or physically attached to your place of business. Work with your customers to strengthen these ties. Make it next to impossible, psychologically, physically and financially, for them to switch to your competitors.

Never take a customer for granted. Be grateful for their business and any future business they may provide.

 *Your Turn*

Complete the following:

- ► List five things you are now doing to provide superior customer service.

- ► List five things you could improve upon where customer service is concerned.

- ► Develop two ways to survey your customers about your level of service. Describe these methods. Write down exactly what information you hope to get from these efforts.

CUSTOMER SERVICE AS A MARKETING TACTIC

Here are seven extremely effective service/marketing techniques you can use to help your business grow and become more profitable, regardless of your competition or current economic conditions. Do not be fooled by their simplicity. The most important thing is that they work, and they work well.

Frequent Buyer Programs

The airlines have frequent flyer programs to reward their best customers. Have a *frequent buyer* program to reward those customers who buy from you on a regular or ongoing basis. It is up to you to define what frequent buying means. Is it the number of purchases, the costs of the individual or cumulative purchases, or is it how many different family members buy from you? Once you define frequent buyer, you can develop the reward program.

The rewards do not have to be expensive or lavish. They should just have a high perceived value, to show the customer you truly appreciate their business. You may want to make it a tiered program, so customers with different buying habits can benefit from the program. A tiered frequent buyer program means that the rewards are different for each successive level of purchase. Whatever you do, it should not be difficult for your regular customers to benefit from this program.

A great example of this type of program is the yogurt store that punches a card for you when you make a purchase. After your tenth or twelfth purchase, the store gives you a free yogurt or something else as a discount. The store uses this program to encourage you to keep coming back and to create a sense of loyalty in you. With this type of program, everyone wins. The store gets more revenue, customers get rewarded for positive behaviors—which are then reinforced and become highly likely to occur again—and both the store and the customer win, because they begin to build a relationship. How do you like doing business where everybody knows your name?

Frequent Referral Programs

The reward structure of *frequent referral programs* is often similar to those of frequent buyer programs, except the rewards are based on the number of referrals a customer makes to your business. Since every small business depends somewhat or entirely on referrals, reward the customers who make referrals to you. Your rewards reinforce their behavior, so they will do it again to get more rewards. This creates a positive cycle and a mutually beneficial relationship.

The frequent referral reward program should be developed in tiers, or levels, in the same manner as the frequent buyer program. A customer who refers to you receives rewards based on the number of referrals. For example, you may simply send the person a thank-you card for the first referral. After the second referral, you make a personal telephone call. When the customer makes a third referral, you give them a small, inexpensive gift that has some perceived value. The fourth referral may earn them a floral arrangement or a gift certificate to your store. The fifth referral should be rewarded with a dinner gift certificate to a very nice restaurant. Then you can start the entire process all over again.

You can use these suggestions as they are, modify them, or develop some of your own. The most important thing is to reward the people who refer new customers to you. When you reinforce their behavior and make them feel good, they will continue to refer because you acknowledged their efforts by showing your appreciation.

Here is another suggestion. Before you use it, make certain your referral sources do not mind having their name visible in your store or office. It is an excellent technique for professionals such as physicians, attorneys and accountants. You can adapt it to your business also.

Create a *Referral Thank You Bulletin Board*. Place the names of your customers on this board each month, whenever they refer new people to you. You can also put the number of referrals they have made. People love to see their name in print on something, and this gives them additional satisfaction because you are showing you appreciate their efforts.

Take this a step further and create a *New Customer Welcome Bulletin Board*. List the names of all your new customers each month, under a message that thanks them for doing business with you. When new customers see that you care enough to put their names up for everyone else to see, they will go out of their way to help you make your small business successful. This is also a primary step in a customer retention program.

Thank You Cards

Thank-you cards are one of the most effective customer service marketing and customer retention techniques you can use, yet not enough small businesses send them out. It only takes a little extra effort on your part to write out a card, address an envelope and send it to someone who has done business with you. It is the best postage stamp marketing investment you can make.

Thank-you cards can be handwritten every time you need to send one, or you can have them preprinted with a message that shows your appreciation. It is even more effective if you develop part of your customer service and retention program around a series of these cards.

Here is an example of a series of cards you can send out to show customers you appreciate their business. You can make them up at your local printer or purchase them from a specialty dealer. Send out the cards in this order: 1) Thank you for your business; 2) Our customers are number one; and when the job is completed, if you are a service provider, 3) It was a pleasure working with you. When I receive a referral, I send out a referral thank-you card or a personal note to the referral source. All this information and the dates the cards are sent are tracked in my customer database.

There is a way for you to extend this thank-you card service marketing program, and that is to include holiday and birthday cards as part of your regular mailings to customers. They will appreciate receiving these other cards from you. It is just another way for you to show you care about them. And do not worry—they will respond with additional purchases and new referrals.

Newsletters and Letters of News

Newsletters are an excellent way to keep your customers informed about business. If you write the newsletter personally, you can provide them with whatever information you want them to have or know. And, because it is coming from you free of charge, they will probably read every word of it. (That is right, free. Never charge customers for your business newsletter, unless you are in the business of publishing and selling a newsletter.)

You can keep your customers involved with your business by promoting contests, sweepstakes, promotions, giveaways or other activities in the newsletter. Then make it so they have to come to your office or store to win the contest. When they arrive, give them whatever they have won and make every effort to solidify their loyalty. Do whatever it takes to retain them as customers. If it is a prospect who has come to see you, do everything you can, from a service perspective, to convert this person to a customer.

If you want to put a twist on the newsletter concept, here is a great variation. And, this may get read faster and be kept longer than a traditional newsletter. It is the letter of news.

You write a personal letter to each customer. Use a computerized customer database to make this task very easy. Two of the best programs I have found are ACT! from Contact Software International (1840 Hutton, #200, Carrollton, Texas 75006, 800-365-0606) and Commence by Jenson-Jones, Inc. (Parkway 109 Office Center, 328 Newman Springs Rd., Red Bank, NJ 07701, 800-289-1548). You use these programs to type in all your customers, create the letter of news, then merge the letter with your customers' names, so the mailing piece is highly personalized.

When you write this letter of news, cover all the same items you would in a newsletter. Use subheadings in this personal letter as you would article headings in the newsletter; feel free to bold your subheadings or important pieces of information. Your customers will be very pleased that you took the time to write them a personal letter, and will probably read every word of it, especially if you keep it to one or two pages. But, if you have a lot to say and you keep it interesting, they will read every word you write.

Consider the letter of news as an alternative to a typical and traditional newsletter.

Telephone Recalls

Telephone recalls or *confirmation calls* are excellent service marketing tools in any business where appointments are necessary. The fact that you have taken the time to call and provide this reminder is perceived as an extra touch of service.

To make your recall program work, call your customers a day in advance to remind them of their appointment or of an event. If certain customers have not been in to see you in quite some time, call them to see how they are doing and inform them of a reason to come in now to do business with you.

Here are three basic telephone customer service hints to help you improve on the phone.

1. Always answer the phone by the third or fourth ring. Give the name of your company and your name.

2. Never put a caller on hold without first asking permission to place them on hold, and never for more than 30 seconds. Then, come back to them to tell them how much longer you will be. If you have a voice mail system or an automated attendant, have the voice tell the caller the approximate waiting time on hold. You might be surprised how much they will appreciate this extra effort from you.

3. If your customers complain that they have trouble getting through to you on the telephone, it may be time to install more telephone lines or numbers. You may even want to consider a toll-free 800 number, since the rates are now very respectable for small business owners.

4. Make telephone recalls at respectable times and ask if it is a good time to talk. If not, ask them when you should call back. They will appreciate your courtesy and politeness.

Reward and Recognition Programs

The concept has already been mentioned several times, especially in relation to frequent buyer and frequent referral programs. Positive reinforcement motivates people to engage repeatedly in the same behavior that was rewarded. Find out what types of rewards your employees and customers want, decide how you will recognize their efforts, and give out the appropriate rewards. Your reward and recognition programs will be even more effective if they come at unexpected times.

Unexpected rewards and recognition are among the most powerful motivators and reinforcers of human behavior. Remember to acknowledge and reward the small accomplishments, just as you do the major wins. Everybody likes to have their back patted and their ego stroked. The better you do this, the more profitable you will be, since people will tell other people to buy products and services from you.

Walk Your Talk

Many of the problems with providing customer and marketing customer service in this country stem from the fact that most businesses only give lip service to customer service. You cannot do that if you want to keep your competitive edge and keep your customers for life. You have to get out and be seen by your staff and your customers. Be a role model of excellent service. Do whatever it takes to service, satisfy and retain your customers. Help your employees in every way possible, so they can do their job better. Treat your staff like royalty and they will, in turn, treat your customers like royalty.

Your visibility is critical to the success of your service/marketing program. Use customer service as a marketing tool, then use the seven techniques mentioned earlier to go beyond customer service, to achieve total customer satisfaction. But, you cannot stop here. The smiling faces of your customers do not mean they are truly satisfied. The only way you will know if you are satisfying your customers is to ask them.

Measuring Customer Satisfaction

Customer satisfaction measurement seems to be the stepchild of marketing and customer service in small businesses. A few businesses take some measurements, but many of them do not know what to do with their information. A former client of mine conducted customer surveys on a quarterly basis. These were simply one-page questionnaires that were mailed to the customer with a stamped return envelope and a letter, requesting the customer fill out the survey and return it. When the business got the surveys back, they read them over and then filed them. When I asked the owner why they were doing this with the information, she told me, "I don't know. I only do surveys because my competitors are doing them. I guess it must be worth something if everyone else is doing it." Does her answer frighten you? It certainly scares me.

If you send out, or conduct, customer satisfaction surveys, do something with the information that you get back. Make improvements or other changes that your customers recommend. Create charts and graphs so you can track your progress against past performance.

Measure everything that you want to have done and improved. Make the results visible for the entire staff. Remember, what gets measured gets done. So if you want to service your customers and make sure they are satisfied, measure and analyze your efforts. Use both quantitative (survey scores) and qualitative (interviews) data. Determine what the information means, and share it with your staff members. They will provide better service if they know in what areas they need to improve.

If you need more help on measuring customer satisfaction, refer to my book, *Measuring Customer Satisfaction,* by Crisp Publications.

Remember that Superior Customer Service Includes Quality

Every business talks about customer service and these same people also talk about quality. Unfortunately, most small business owners do not know that much about service quality improvement and are, therefore, unable to take customer service in their businesses to the next level.

There are two simple ways to improve quality in your business. First, ask your customers—they are the ones who ultimately define service quality anyway. Ask them what you need to do. Second, measure everything you do every day so that you are constantly working to improve your quality. Do not try to do one thing 100% better. Do 100 things 1% better, every day. For example, a $\frac{1}{2}$% improvement in the service performance of your staff every week makes you about 25% better by the end of one year. Now that is what I call service improvement.

Service quality improvement and customer service are not one-time things. You do not just do them first and forget them for years to come. They both require an ongoing process of never-ending, continuous improvement. Your superior levels of customer service and service quality improvement begin with a commitment by you, the owner, to a new philosophy of doing business and a new attitude toward employees and customers. Find out exactly what customers need and expect from you, give it to them and then discover ways you can go beyond that type of customer service to excite and delight your customers. All it takes is a little common sense and a little bit of extra effort.

ASK YOURSELF

▶ Describe the customer service marketing techniques you are now using. Which new ones will you begin to use within the next three months?

▶ How do you track customer complaints? How do you respond to customers' suggestions about improving your business?

▶ Discuss your employees' customer service skills.

▶ What else can you do to improve the service quality of your business or organization?

▶ How do you measure customer satisfaction and service quality improvement?

CHAPTER TWELVE

NEVER FORGET
YOUR BACK END

DON'T MISS YOUR GREATEST MONEY-MAKING OPPOR-TUNITY

Too many small business owners are so concerned with daily sales and up-front cash and profits that they miss the greatest money-making opportunity in their business. That opportunity is their back-end marketing and sales program.

Back-end marketing means going back to your customers to sell them additional products and services, time and again. You let them know when you are selling something at a reduced price, providing an ancillary product or service to your current line or offering a new product or service. You let them know this as soon as you can, because they are more likely to buy from you than new customers or prospects you are trying to turn into customers.

Your back-end marketing program is most effective when you know exactly who your customers are and what their lifetime value to you is worth. For example, if you sell a product that costs a customer $10 and they have to buy it every month, they will spend $120 with you each year. If you figure that you can keep them as loyal customers for 10 years—theoretical lifetime—the lifetime value of each individual customer is $1,200. This is just the direct lifetime value, or marginal net worth, of the customer to you. The figure is usually higher, because the customer either buys more or begins to refer new customers to you. In any case, you can actually spend more to get that new customer than you previously thought.

So, you know who your customer is and what he or she is worth to your business. Now, you have to increase that lifetime value by getting each customer to buy more, trade up, be up-sold or cross-sold. Here is how you do it.

STARTING YOUR BACK-END MARKETING PROGRAM

The first thing you do is provide excellent customer service to everyone who buys from you. You cannot make a back-end sale if the customer is not happy with his or her original purchase. Make sure you give everyone great service by following the suggestions in Chapter 11.

Start out giving great service by providing the customer with postpurchase reassurance. Most small business owners, and especially sales professionals, are familiar with postpurchase dissonance (PPD). This is when a buyer feels remorse about making a purchase. It is up to you to reassure the buyer that the decision to buy, and the actual purchase, was a good one.

Do this immediately if the purchase was made face to face; then you can try to up-sell or cross-sell them something else that is complementary to what they have just bought. Otherwise, call the customer on the phone the day after the purchase was made. Tell the customer he or she made an excellent decision on their purchase. Remind the customer that you will always be there to provide whatever service they may need. Then, follow the call with a letter restating your reassurance of their purchase and exactly what you plan to do to keep them satisfied. If you have to ship a product to a customer, include a little note separate from the the letter, reminding them of these same things. Constantly reassure them that their decision to do business with you was a smart one and that you will do everything possible to keep them satisfied.

Your postpurchase reassurance efforts pave the way for a successful back-end marketing program. This is your first step to building long-term customer loyalty. Now, back up a little bit and think about something else. That is, should you take a smaller profit or even a loss on the initial purchase if the back-end potential is tremendous? I think you should. Regardless of the type or amount of initial purchase, provide the same high level of post purchase reassurance.

Several years ago, I had a client who wanted to introduce a new product. The product sold for less than $10. He wanted to advertise the product heavily and create top-of-mind aware-ness with his target market, so customers would start buying and continue to buy. I suggested he take an initial loss on the product and consider the back-end possibilities.

We put pencil to paper and figured out that the product cost him less than $3 to produce. If he gave it away for an initial purchase and he could get it into the hands of just 1,000 prospective customers, we would be operating at a $3,000 loss to start out. We did this, and the 1,000 customers loved the product. Not only did they buy more, but they began referring the product to their friends. Soon, everyone who was anyone in that particular industry was either using the product or at least had heard of it. Sales went from $250,000 per year to $1.5 million in less than three years. All from a product that sold for under $10.

The power of the back-end is phenomenal.

Now, you have decided either to sell your product or service at full price, give it away or take a slight loss on the initial sale. The important thing is that you have made the initial sale. You are ready to begin your back-end marketing program.

Send a long, informative and easy-to-read sales letter to your customers about another product or an ancillary product to one they bought. Tell them of the benefits of having this product. Basically, make sure your letter is a salesperson in print.

Several of your customers will buy on this second round of selling. Later on, go back to all of them to sell them something else. Continue in this manner until the sales from your letters or other direct mail pieces no longer pay for themselves. When you market in this manner, consider putting a special bonus in your letter for the customer who refers new customers to you. This may get your original customer to buy and may motivate them to get people they know to buy from you also.

Two Great Twists on Back End Marketing

There are times when you have exactly what the prospect wants, but he or she does not want to spend the money. No matter what you do to make the sale, it is just not going to happen. Here is how to make the sale and start a back-end program simultaneously.

Offer different versions of your product or service. Give prospects the chance to buy a good, better and best model. When they have a choice, there is a greater possibility that you will get them as a customer. Ironically, most people buy the middle priced item. Now, you can start selling them ancillary products or services in the price range they want, while at the same time giving them great customer service.

The second great twist takes courage. If you do not have something a prospect wants, sell them something from your competitors. You can always find a competitor who has the product or service in the price range, with just the right bells and whistles that the prospect wants. Sell your competitor's product. Then begin your back-end marketing program.

You are probably thinking that I am crazy for telling you to sell your potential customer something from your competitor. But, think about it. You go to your competitor and tell him or her that you will sell your customers their products or services and that you want a piece of the sale. They would have to be crazy to turn away the business. You are making some initial money, and both of you are gaining a customer.

Whichever of these methods you try, they start you off on your back-end marketing program.

OTHER TYPES OF BACK-END MARKETING PROGRAMS

Here are some of the best back-end marketing programs I have come across and used. See if you can adapt them for your small business:

- ▶ **Customized Accessories.** Your customer has just purchased something from you; you have made sure they are happy with the purchase. You contact them to tell them that you have a customized accessory with their name on it that goes along perfectly with the item they just purchased, or provide them with certain accessories that enhance the psychological and financial value of their original purchase.

- ▶ **Up-Sell or Cross-Sell Higher Quality Items.** When your customers are satisfied with their purchase, go back to them and inform them of a newer or better version of what they have. Show them the benefits of having the higher quality item. Tell them how they will look better, feel better, work faster, have less stress, or whatever, but they need to purchase the higher quality item from you soon.

▶ **Package Inserts.** These fliers or order forms make great little riders when you ship the original purchase. If the purchase is over the counter, slip these fliers into the bag or box. The items they are promoting can be related to the original purchase, or they can be totally unrelated. The goal here is to get the information into the customer's hands so he or she can make a decision to buy at a later date.

▶ **Till Further Notice (TFN) or Continuity Series.** This is where you will keep sending products to the customer and invoicing them, charging their credit card or making an electronic funds transfer until they tell you to cancel the program. Often, the initial sale in a continuity series back-end program is made at significant discount, at a loss or even for free, to ensure the customer's participation in the program. You see these continuity series programs with book clubs, record clubs, magazine subscriptions and health club memberships. Figure out a way to adapt it to your business, and watch the bottom line grow.

▶ **Negative Options.** Customers participate in a buying program that requires them to send in a card or make a call, to tell the company they do not want the purchase for that month. Otherwise, the purchase is sent. The negative options program requires the customer to make the effort to stop the sale, and that is why many book and record clubs use this approach.

▶ **Positive Options.** This is very similar to the negative options approach, except that the customer will not receive a product unless he or she returns a card requesting the product.

▶ **Free Drawing.** Have all your customers enter a contest for a free drawing. You must give away one grand prize. Send all the "losers" a letter telling them they did not win the grand prize, but they did win a valuable second prize. Make that second prize something that can result in additional sales. A restaurant did this and told the "losers" to come in for dinner; the restaurant owner would buy that person's dinner, and the dessert for the entire dinner party. You can also put several twists on this.

Your Turn

Answer the following:

► What is the purpose and central principle of a back end marketing program?

► What types of businesses benefit from back end marketing?

► Describe the benefits of back-end marketing programs that would be effective in your business.

MISTAKES PEOPLE MAKE WITH BACK END MARKETING

The most glaring mistake people make in back-end marketing is not having a program at all. This is hard to believe when you consider that more money can be made on the back-end than on the front-end.

The second biggest mistake is not capturing the names and addresses of all customers. This means that every small business owner, including retailers, should get their customers' names and addresses for future selling opportunities. If you cannot get the information at the time of purchase, invite them to fill out a card for a contest or drawing. Do whatever it takes to get this information.

The third mistake is not going back often enough to the same customer. This happens when customers make a second or third purchase, and the small business owner arbitrarily decides they will not purchase again. You do not know that. Go back to them as often as you have something to sell them, and as long as they keep buying something or showing interest. Stop going back to them only when they tell you to or when the mailings are not paying for themselves.

The fourth mistake, which can be deadly, is not believing the back-end marketing program can be profitable. The result is usually that the business owner assigns a junior person to handle the program. Never, ever do this. Your back-end marketing program is too important and can be too profitable to leave it in the hands of just anybody.

The fifth biggest mistake is not finding something to sell on the back-end. If you have a one-shot product or service, you can still develop a back-end program. Find things from competitors that you can sell. Find items from noncompetitors that you can sell. Create special reports or information pieces that you can sell. Sell seminars or booklets. The ideas for what you can sell are limited only by your desire to find something to sell on the back-end.

From Back to Front and Back Again

There may be times when a customer does not want what you are selling and does not want what you can sell them from a competitor. However, since you have a back-end program, you have lots of other things to sell. Take some of these back-end items and move them to the front of the line. Try to sell them to the customers just to make your initial sale and to capture the customer's name and address. After the back-end becomes the front end, you can go back to your original back-end program and build on the initial sale.

ASK YOURSELF

► What back-end marketing programs do you have in effect?

► What else could you do in terms of back-end marketing?

► What back-end marketing programs do you plan to implement? What benefits do you anticipate?

CHAPTER THIRTEEN

YOUR GUIDE TO SMALL BUSINESS SUCCESS

BASIC MARKET- ING PLANS

Small business owners need a marketing plan to succeed. There are no two ways about it. Without a plan, a roadmap, how would you know how to get where you want to go?

The purpose of this chapter and the next is to help you gain marketing skills, in addition to the technical and professional skills you possess. The marketing plan is the first step.

All marketing plans contain the same basic information. There is material on the business, its history, goals and objectives; customers and their needs, wants and expectations; competitors and their marketing programs; plans to advertise and promote the business. The main difference between plans is whether it is to be a brief marketing plan or an extensive, comprehensive marketing plan.

The two tables that follow show you how to write a one-page marketing plan or a slightly more expanded, quick and easy marketing plan. Marketing plans are never truly quick and easy; I am calling it that to differentiate the brief plan from the comprehensive plan.

The remainder of this chapter focuses on how to write a comprehensive marketing plan. If you have never written one, follow the guidelines and recommendations. Write one comprehensive marketing plan at least every three to five years in your small business. Develop the shorter versions in between, and you will provide yourself with a roadmap for success.

One-Page Marketing Plan

Project _____ Date _____

1. Goals and Objectives: Short-term and Long-term

2. Target Market Characteristics: Age, Gender, Income, etc.

3. Target Market Needs

4. Your Strengths, Weaknesses, Opportunities and Threats

5. Competitors' Strengths, Weaknesses, Opportunities and Threats

6. Your Competitive Position and How You Will Compete

7. Marketing and Advertising Budget

8. Promotional Strategies

9. Tactical Action Plans

10. Program Execution and Responsibilities

Quick And Easy Marketing Plan Contents

1. MARKET ANALYSIS

- Market Business Analysis
- Company SWOT Analysis*
- Competitors' Comparative Characteristics
- Customer Analysis: Target Market Characteristics

2. STRATEGY DEVELOPMENT

- Project Mission Statement
- Goals: Primary/Secondary, Short-term/Long-term
- Objectives
- Strategies to Achieve Objectives

3. PLAN IMPLEMENTATION

- Tactics Development
- Marketing Action Plan for Each Goal and Associated Objectives
- Project Completion Schedule
- Advertising Cost Plan

4. PROGRAM EVALUATION AND FOLLOW-UP

- Goal Achievement: Yes/No, Why?
- Image/Awareness Surveys
- Customer Satisfaction Survey
- Other Feedback

---

* See Company Analysis for discussion of SWOT Analysis.

SMALL BUSINESS OWNERS, THEIR CLIENTS AND CUSTOMERS

It is imperative that you understand the concept and definition of marketing before actually writing a marketing plan or developing a business marketing campaign. Marketing is more than sales, advertising, promotion and public relations. The textbook definition of marketing is *the exchange of activities (goods, products, programs and services), at an agreed upon price, completed for the purpose of satisfying customers' needs and achieving marketers' goals.* This means that a business and a client are involved in the voluntary exchange of a product or service, usually with a cost incurred by the client, and both benefit from the exchange. The exchange occurs through some channel of distribution—marketplace, office, etc.—as a result of a communication process—advertising, promotion or referral—that transpired prior to the visit. That is the textbook definition.

The real-world definition of marketing is *the business sells customers what they want, at a price they are willing to pay and the business makes a profit.* After all, why would you sell anything at less than a profit for your business, unless you are using the product or service as a loss leader?

The key factor in your marketing relationship is your ability, as the small business owner, to identify, through market analysis and strategic market planning techniques, client needs that must be satisfied. It is then up to you to develop services or programs to satisfy those needs, so customers come to you, rather than to a competitor.

At the same time, you maintain existing services, positioning your business so it will be viewed favorably by the target customer segments. You develop a mix of strategies to influence customers to purchase your products or services, evaluate the effect of your strategies and tactics on the marketing environment, engage in competition with other small business owners and determine the success or failure of the marketing approach—often measured in repeat purchases, referrals and customer loyalty.

Defining Your Business

Before developing a marketing plan, a small business owner must properly define his or her business. Several questions must be answered during this preliminary phase to ensure that the marketing strategies and tactics are effectively and success-fully carried out. Responses to these inquiries focus the business's marketing plan. You are creating an outline from which the marketing plan will be written.

What is the mission/nature of the business? This answer provides a course of action for the business. Any small business owner, trying to develop or expand a business, is providing a service first and a product or a program second. You must identify the specific products or services you will offer so that the marketing plan can effectively promote these to customers.

What image (reputation) will the business have? Every small business owner presents an image of him or herself first and the business second. Their dress, speech and interactions with others determine what customers think of their image. Image also affects whether or not customers return for future services.

Always be professional, courteous, friendly, prompt and neat, and follow up with all customers. Make sure your staff does the same. This will ensure that you develop a positive image and reputation with your customers.

What products or services will you offer? Clearly define what you will provide for customers. If you are a general small business, let them know. If you are highly specialized, tell them that also. Give them a list and description of the services and programs you can provide and how these will benefit them.

Who are the customers and where are they located? Identify where you will draw your customers from. Describe their distinguishing characteristics and where they live and work. How will your services be presented? Is your location convenient and accessible? You must know your customers to serve them well.

What unique positioning does your business hold?
Describe what makes your business different and unique. Tell why customers should come to you, rather than go to someone else. Describe the benefits customers receive from your unique business.

When and how will you distribute products or services?
Offer products or services only when you are fully ready. Determine whether you will see customers at their office or they will come to you. However and wherever you do business, remember to make it accessible and convenient for your customers. This includes when you set your business hours.

What are the financial requirements of your business?
Perhaps this question should be answered first—the response may determine whether or not you will go into business. Financial planning must be completed, including start-up costs, operational expenses, revenue projections, cash flow estimates, marketing and advertising costs and methods of payment. Plan your cash flow needs according to how customers pay. Proper financial planning will inform you of the availability of money to continue to market the business.

When you have answered these questions, you will have completed the basic analysis of your small business. Your answers will guide you in developing a comprehensive, written marketing plan. Although the developmental process may seem long and tedious, it is necessary to compete successfully with other small business owners and to maintain a profitable business. The table on the next page shows the basic information included in a marketing plan. It is followed by an expanded table of contents for your marketing plan. Use these as guides to develop your comprehensive marketing plan. They will serve as a foundation for how you run your business.

Basic Marketing Plan Components

The basic premise of your marketing program can be quickly and easily communicated by describing the items listed below.

1. Philosophy and mission of your products or services business

2. Goals and objectives of your products or services business

3. Provision, quality and scope of your products or services

4. Differentiation of your service from competitors', including positioning of your business

5. Market and work environment, including your business' and those of competitors

6. Financial goals of your business

7. Client behaviors, intentions and needs

8. Company strengths and weaknesses

9. Competitors' strengths and weaknesses

10. Client/customer service approach

11. Target markets and market segmentation procedures

12. Promotional programs

13. Business management and client service procedures

14. Provisions for responding effectively to change, including marketing and financial alternatives

15. Expansion and growth opportunities

Comprehensive Marketing Plan
Table of Contents

I. *Executive Summary*
1. Description and rationale for the marketing plan
2. Introduction to program or service
3. Anticipated audience, sales and profits
4. Competitive position/market niche/market share

II. *Market Analysis/Situational Analysis*
1. Market research results
2. Market demand/attractiveness analysis
3. Product Life Cycle (PLC) stage and analysis
4. Company analysis
5. Competitor analysis
6. Product/program/service analysis

III. *Market Segmentation Procedures/Customer Analysis*
1. Target market selection criteria
2. Customer characteristics
3. Customer needs and wants
4. Product/program/service-customer fit

IV. *Marketing Mix: Strategies and Tactics*
1. Business goals and financial performance
2. Marketing objectives: niche, position, advantages
3. Marketing strategies: corporate, business, PLC
4. Marketing tactics: action plans, implementation

V. *Promotional Mix*
1. Advertising program: description of media schedule
2. Publicity/public relations
3. Direct sales
4. Sales promotions

VI. *Marketing Results*
1. Evaluation of marketing efforts
2. Sales and profits
3. Achievement of goals and differential advantage
4. Recommendations for future opportunities

VII. *Marketing Support Documents*
1. Budgets: income, expense, advertising, publicity
2. Advertising copy, layout and graphics
3. Forms and charts
4. Legal documents and required approvals

MARKET ANALYSIS

Your marketing plan should be based on sound information about the marketplace, developed through market analysis that includes basic market research techniques. Carefully and thoroughly, you analyze your own business, the business of competitors and the characteristics and needs of prospective customers.

Market analysis determines the critical path your small business will follow to identify and secure customers, distribute its programs and services, advertise and promote your business, allocate personnel and other resources to specific operational and marketing tasks, determine whether or not it is feasible to try to attract a particular client target market and forecast business revenue goals.

Market analysis begins with a market research study. This will determine the efficacy of opening up, expanding or marketing your small business in a particular area. Market research can include a *feasibility study* to determine if your business would be financially sound, a *needs assessment* of businesses operating in the area to see if they would require your products or services (assuming you are a business-to-business operator) or a *survey of customers* in the area to determine if their needs and buying patterns warrant locating your business near them. You should identify the goals and objectives of your products, programs and services, your justification for offering these services, the cost to the customers, the level of competition for what you are offering and any other critical issues that may influence your business. The rest of the marketing program will be based on the results of the market research and the market analysis.

The importance of the market analysis cannot be overemphasized. A properly conducted and completed analysis will *often* lead to success; a poor analysis will *definitely* lead to failure. Furthermore, the success of your business will come from the marketing plan, based on this market analysis. You must have sound data on which to base your decision. Only a good market study can tell you whether or not opening or expanding your business in a certain area has a good chance of success. Plan to invest time and money into the market analysis. The research will more than pay for itself.

Market Research

Market research is the systematic process of gathering, analyzing, interpreting and utilizing relevant information for the purposes of making accurate marketing decisions regarding your small business. The objectives of this process include understanding customer behavior and perceptions, providing specific, verifiable, hard data about your marketplace, developing and updating your marketing information system, identifying potential customers for your products or services, determining factors that will reduce the risk of offering these products or services and measuring how well previous products or services have been provided and received. Market research is the measurement component of marketing. You will need to conduct it before to developing a marketing program, and again after you implement your plan, to determine its effectiveness.

More simply, market research is asking and finding out what customers want from you and what your competitors are currently doing for their customers. The results of your research help you decide how to compete.

The marketing research process follows five typical steps.

▶ Identifying and defining the problem

▶ Designing a research program

▶ Collecting data

▶ Analyzing and interpreting the data

▶ Solving the problem and recommendations for further action.

Before you begin a market research program, make certain you meet three criteria: 1) you are uncertain about a particular marketing decision; 2) you are prepared to change the direction or focus of your business in response to research results; and 3) research cost will not exceed its potential value to the business. If these criteria are not met, it may not be appropriate for you to do a market research study at this time.

Most business professionals are familiar with market research studies, often called feasibility studies, done prior to opening a business. These studies are designed to determine the financial viability of the project. You check out the location, competition in the area, the potential customer base and buying habits. Be aware that market research is an ongoing process that you must perform regularly after your business opens.

Market research is only as valuable as the actual data that is collected and techniques used to gather that data. Market researchers use both *secondary* and *primary* data in their decision-making process. Secondary data is information that was collected for other purposes than the current project. It is available through external sources such as government publications, competitors' publications, trade associations and publications, libraries, research organizations, universities, census, Dun and Bradstreet reports, sales and marketing surveys, former employees of competitors and customers, newspapers and trade journals.

Primary data is information you collect yourself to analyze a specific situation. The data can be either *qualitative* (subjective) or *quantitative* (measurable). Qualitative data is useful and essential, but cannot be statistically analyzed. It is gathered through focus groups, personal interviews, case studies or open-ended comments to determine customer attitudes and preferences toward your small business.

Quantitative data is more reliable because statistical analyses can be performed on it. Sources include surveys, either in person, on the telephone (telemarketing) or through the mail (direct mail), observation of behaviors with criterion reference points for scoring consumer actions and natural experiments (testing people's reactions in different situations) using objective reference points. The results of the analysis, combined with qualitative primary data and available secondary data sources, will enable you to make a more accurate marketing decision related to your small business.

Advantages to using secondary data include saved time and money and minimized duplication of effort. Disadvantages are that the data may not apply to the situation or that the data may be outdated. Secondary data must be evaluated for its relevancy, credibility and accuracy before it is used to determine if primary data collection must be undertaken. As long as the advantages of using secondary data outweigh the disadvantages and the results point to the necessity of primary research, proceed with your primary data collection.

Perform your marketing research before you develop your marketing program, during the implementation of your program and afterwards as you evaluate the effectiveness of your efforts. Many small business owners neglect to perform research believing it to be too expensive or time consuming. Marketing research costs, in time, money and risk, are usually less than the cost of not doing market research and proceeding without support information—and having the new business or product/service offering blow up in your face.

It is always cheaper to pay up front, as a preventative measure, than, later on, to fix a problem. If you think you cannot afford market research, remember that you cannot afford *not* to do the research for your marketing plan.

The results of market research are usually described in a market research report and in the marketing plan. A separate market research study should be undertaken for each project. Never start a new project with old information or information that is not applicable. This will eliminate possible confusion in future studies, and each individual report can serve as a future, secondary data source.

It is usually better for a small business owner to hire a professional market research firm, rather than perform the study alone. These firms have the data collection and statistical analysis capabilities to do the job. The investment will be worth it.

If you don't want to spend the money, go out on the street. Ask 50 to 100 people what they think of the product or service you plan to sell. Ask them how they will use it, what benefits they see in it, and what they are willing to pay for it. This will give you a representative sample from which to determine whether or not you should proceed.

COMPANY ANALYSIS

Small business owners must first comprehensively analyze their businesses before successfully marketing their products or services to customers. This analysis requires taking a very critical and objective look at their entire business, including the roles of all staff members, the business's financial goals and operating procedures.

The simplest way to analyze your small business is called a SWOT analysis. SWOT stands for *Strengths, Weaknesses, Opportunities* and *Threats.* It identifies the small business owner's or business's:

► **S**trengths, such as a large customer volume, quality customer service, financial support or personnel

► **W**eaknesses, such as lack of capital, a competitor located close by who has a large customer base or your lack of customers

► **O**pportunities available for successful performance, such as better customer handling, more personal service, increased business growth in the area, increased need for your products or services, possibly coupled with the fact that no other small business owner in the area is delivering the same type of service, or a competitor who is going out of business.

► **T**hreats, such as competitors having lower-priced programs and services, other new small businesses opening up or unrealistic performance goals.

These are some of the possible components of a SWOT analysis. Of course, others can be included. This analysis should serve as the basis for a more comprehensive company analysis. Use the chart that follows to develop your SWOT analysis.

You must remain objective, both during the SWOT analysis and during the comprehensive analysis that follows it. It is sometimes difficult to analyze your own business objectively. One suggestion is to imagine your business as your biggest competitor's. What would you look for and how would you

SWOT Analysis

STRENGTHS	WEAKNESSES

OPPORTUNITIES	THREATS

use that information to your advantage? Extend the analysis of your business to include descriptions of the following information, which is also necessary to formulate a successful marketing program:

► **Historical Data:** How and why your business was formed, the rationale behind its formation, the reasons it is in business, how well it has or is projected to perform and the philosophical perspectives that led to its formation.

► **Products and Services:** The marketable products and services you will provide for customers. Describe each in detail so you can develop a marketing and promotion strategy for each one.

► **Markets:** A brief description of who you expect your customers to be, any unique characteristics they may possess and why they would buy your products or services.

► **Technology Position:** Decide upon and describe the level of sophistication of your business. If your technology is highly sophisticated, this will be used in the marketing campaign to position your business at the forefront of the most recent advances in your business or industry.

► **Operational Resources:** All the resources, including internal personnel, external suppliers and vendors, and available money that can be used to provide your products or services to customers.

► **Competitors:** Describe your closest competitors—those small business owners who provide similar programs and services. Analyze their strengths and weaknesses. You can do this through a SWOT analysis that you perform on them, financial and stock reports, sales reports, available personnel and archival data. Determine each competitor's relative position in the marketplace; use their market position and apparent weaknesses to position your business better and to make your marketing program more effective.

► **Customers:** Describe everything you need to know about your customers. As a consultant for small businesses, I have found this to be the least developed section of their marketing plans. Pay close attention to this critical aspect of your business.

► **Success Factors:** Identify key factors for the success of your business. These will include finances, programs and services or staff performance. Consider customer evaluation criteria: what they use to determine if they will buy from you.

► **Cost Comparison:** Identify the pricing relationships among your competitors. Compare those with the prices you plan for similar offerings.

► **Competitive Position:** The position you hold in the marketplace is based on the relative position of your competitors. Be aware of what you have done to achieve this position, what you must do to maintain it, and how you can try to improve it.

Your competitive position and relative market share in comparison to your three biggest competitors will influence greatly the types of marketing strategies you develop. Determine if you are the market leader, one of several followers, a market challenger, are new to your marketplace or a niche marketer.

A strong competitive position within a small market niche is sometimes more desirable for a small business than a large market share. Try to achieve the former; either be the big fish in a little pond or build your own pond. You gain a competitive advantage through lower costs for services, high quality of service and follow-up and proper positioning within a unique market niche. Once you are established and successful, you can expand your business.

Just because something gave you a competitive advantage in one location does not mean it will work in a second or third location. Consider each expansion of of your business as a separate marketing effort, a separate attempt to gain a new competitive position.

COMPETITOR ANALYSIS

Investigation of other competitors is one of the most important components of a market analysis. No matter how qualified to provide business services to customers small business owners are, they cannot succeed in the marketplace without knowing the competitors and their capabilities. Gather information to monitor the current competition, identify their strengths and weaknesses, and predict the entrance of new competitors. Include businesses whose opening in your area would infringe on your customer base. Every small business owner should develop a profile of significant competitors. The first step is to be aware that competitors within your marketplace share common characteristics, such as location, equipment, vendors and even customers. Collect as much information on the competition as possible.

Many readily available sources of this information exist. These include newspaper articles about the competition, trade shows and professional associations, suppliers and vendors, trade magazines, previous employees of competitors, related business and social contacts, customer/customer service information, new product/program/service announcements and brochures and advertising and promotional campaigns. These are the most readily available sources and are easiest to access.

Once you gather the information, you must develop a competitive profile. Write it with detailed descriptions of their operations and marketing plans as you know them. You must know how your competitors operate, how they service their customers, what they plan to do to market their businesses, what their fees or prices are for specific products, services and programs and any other strengths or weakness they may have. Competitor information will also help you position your small business in relation to their businesses, so you will know if you are the leader, a follower or a market challenger. This will help you develop your marketing strategies. Finally, when you are certain you have collected all the accurate information you need about your competitors, develop your marketing plan for your small business.

The best and least expensive way to get all this information is to shop your competitors. Visit them personally. See how they treat you, the customer. Call them on the phone. Listen to how they respond to your questions. Have family and friends do the same thing. Compare notes with them. Check your own business the same way. What are your competitors doing that you are not? Is it good or bad? Do customers like it or dislike it? What can you do to take customers away from your competitors? What weaknesses do they have that you can capitalize on? Answer these questions and you will be way ahead.

CUSTOMER ANALYSIS

The customer analysis represents an attempt to identify the potential needs of prospective customers, and how your business can satisfy those needs. The simplest way to do this is to use the three column *Customer Analysis* chart below.

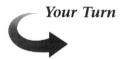 *Your Turn*   ***Complete each column below and determine where the best matches are between what they need and what you provide. Then, fill in the*** Target Market Characteristics ***chart to help you more accurately define your customer base.***

Customer Analysis Chart

Customer Needs	Business Features	Business Benefits
_____	_____	_____
_____	_____	_____
_____	_____	_____
_____	_____	_____
_____	_____	_____

Target Market Characteristics

Characteristic	Primary	Secondary
Location	_____	_____
Age	_____	_____
Gender	_____	_____
Income	_____	_____
Education	_____	_____
Occupation	_____	_____
Marital Status	_____	_____
Family Size	_____	_____
Family Life Cycle	_____	_____
Buying Influences	_____	_____
Benefits Sought	_____	_____
User Status	_____	_____
Usage Rate	_____	_____
Loyalty Status	_____	_____
Attitudes	_____	_____
Readiness State	_____	_____
Race/Religion/Nationality	_____	_____
Lifestyle	_____	_____
Social Class	_____	_____
Personality	_____	_____

I strongly believe that, the more you know about your customers, the better your chances for success. This will be true even if you omit any other portion of the marketing analysis. You will still have to conduct market research to find out about your customers and use the information to create your marketing plan.

MARKET BARRIERS, MARKET DEMAND AND MARKET SHARE

Market Barriers

Several barriers both to market entry and market exit must be identified. Some of the entry barriers include the minimum size or number of resources your small business must have for a cost-effective operation, the differentiation of programs and services from competitors within each market segment and the customer's perception that your small business is unique. Financial requirements can also serve as barriers to market entry. These include expenditures for facilities, equipment, furniture, proposed operating costs and advertising. Other barriers you should consider include costs incurred by customers when they have to switch from one small business to another, cost disadvantages of being a new entrant in the marketplace—which may mean all your costs are higher than anyone else who has been in business for a period of time—and laws governing licensing and operating your small business.

Barriers to market entry are counterbalanced by barriers to market exit. Market exit occurs when a small business is no longer profitable, due to high delivery costs or oversaturation of the market by competitors. A major barrier to market exit is a strong desire by the small business owner to continue with a business, despite a decline in customers, revenue or profits. Good business sense would suggest that the business be sold at this time. Perhaps another small business owner could build it back up and make it work.

Market Demand

Over the years, many significant changes in the demand for products and services usually occur. More and more, consumers are becoming educated about their needs; they want the best value for their money. Others may be shopping around for the best price, regardless of value or service. It is especially important for you to be aware of the demand characteristics of the marketplace so that your marketing, sales and customer service approaches can be properly aligned with what is needed and wanted by customers and with what the competition is doing.

PREDICTING MARKET REVENUE

Market Revenue

This is the predicted dollar amount that a business expects to earn within a given time frame, when it provides products and services to a specific target market. The time frame is usually one year. However, small business owners would be wise to consider the *lifetime* value of a customer to the business and treat that customer accordingly. For example, if a customer will spend $1,000 with you during one year, that customer is worth $10,000 over 10 years—more if they stay with you longer or require more products and services. Consider your market revenue projections for a shorter time span, and consider your customer's revenue value over a lifetime. Then, give them the service they deserve, as if they were making a lifetime value purchase each time they do business with you.

To predict market revenue, you obviously need to know the price of your products and services. While there are many pricing formulas, as well as comparative or competitive pricing based on what established businesses are doing, always take these four factors, the 4-Cs, into consideration when you establish prices.

> ► **Customers:** target market, consumers, clients or customers

▶ **Costs:** resources, products/services development, labor and suppliers

▶ **Competition:** current pricing policies, along with market share and position of competitors

▶ **Controls:** government or public policies and legislation, laws and regulations.

Price strategically and value-based. This guarantees that both the business and the customer will be satisfied with what is being provided for the money.

Selecting Target Markets

The next step in market analysis is to determine the target markets—those customers who will need products and services. The customers are primarily identified by a set of distinguishing characteristics. The more characteristics you use to identify customers, the more you can segment the target market. You will also be better able to identify your best potential customers from within this target market group, through their specific distinguishing characteristics. Then you can segment the target market according to those characteristics. This helps determine exactly what types of marketing, advertising and promotional programs you must use to reach the target market.

MARKET SEGMENTATION

Market segmentation is a process. It begins with the identification of the target market and specifies characteristics for that market. This refinement process enables you to market your small business successfully. You only consider one small group of potential customers at a time, which allows you to target your efforts to a specific portion of the chosen market segment. It leads to the development of more effective marketing strategies and tactics, directed at the best potential purchasers of your products and services.

The following characteristics are recommended for you to use to segment the marketplace.

► **Size:** The size of the potential market can be based on either the total volume of dollar sales or the number of possible customers. The market segment can be broken down further by considering a particular geographic location for the service thrust.

► **Geographic Location:** Customers are situated in a local, county, state, regional or national marketplace. Develop programs with consumer preferences in mind. Sales techniques must reflect the buying behavior of a particular location. Small business owners usually start by marketing their products and services to customers who live or work near them before expanding to other service areas.

► **Demographics:** Potential customers are identified by age, race, religion, nationality, gender, marital status, income, education level, socioeconomic status, occupation, number of people per household, job title, job requirements or leisure behaviors. These are only some of the demographic characteristics that identify customers in a potential marketplace. You can develop others that suit your business.

► **Psychographics (Sociopsychological Needs):** It is possible, and often desirable, to offer products and services according to the attitudes, beliefs, emotional aspects or needs of your customers. Every small business owner should be able to identify a need, want or consumer desire that can be satisfied if the customer purchases one or several products and services. How does what you sell make the customer feel better about himself or herself or raise the customer's self esteem?

► **Purchaser/User Characteristics:** Identify the characteristics of both the purchaser and user. They may not be the same person. A successful small business owner must get to know the purchaser, the user, what they both need and want and how to best satisfy each.

► **Purchaser Influences:** These are the people, places and things that will influence customers in their decision to purchase products and services. Before the customer will come to see you, these influences must be identified, attended to and satisfied. Quite often, small business owners overlook this component of market segmentation. Then they wonder why a customer was lost or never came to them in the first place.

The reason purchaser influences sometimes get lost in the marketing plan is that they may not always be in the forefront of the segmentation analysis. These influences must be found and satisfied to ensure a successful business.

► **Service Usage:** It is unfortunate when small business owners determine who will buy from them based on hours open that are convenient for the owner. When segmenting a market according to usage capabilities, determine if the customers can do business with you during the hours you want to be open. This is not usually the case; consider altering or extending your hours to accommodate customer usage patterns. When you can be flexible, such as by increasing your operating hours, there is a greater possibility that customers will choose to buy from you than from someone less accessible. The point to remember is that convenience and flexibility are almost as important to a customer's decision to buy as the cost of products and services.

► **Buyer Behavior:** Products and services are purchased for a variety of reasons. Small business owners must identify why customers are coming to their business and not going somewhere else. Cost will probably be an important factor in all buying decisions, given the state of the economy and the customer's search for value at a reasonable price. Another important consideration is the method of payment for products and services. Does your business accept personal checks, credit cards or just cash?

It would be very nice and easy if markets could be segmented simply by separating potential targets according to any one of these eight components. It would be ideal for both the beginning and experienced small business owner to identify and segment the target market according to one characteristic and design marketing programs accordingly. However, that is not the case. In your small business, as with most other businesses or industries, the components are never truly separate. They exist in combination, such as market size and buyer behavior, demographics and geographic location or purchaser/user characteristics and purchaser influences and usage patterns.

The interrelationship among all eight becomes increasingly evident and complex as you undertake an in-depth analysis of market segmentation procedures. For this reason, the primary segmentation process must be carried out carefully. Otherwise, you will develop inappropriate marketing programs.

Competition is a secondary characteristic that your small business may want to use to segment its markets—competition either as it currently exists or where the market segment is small and *lacks* competition. This is a good starting point for all new small business owners. It allows them to make a name themselves without worrying about other competitors.

You can also segment a market based on its *potential growth*, where the segments are expanding at a quick rate; *value*, where the customers will pay enough for products and services you are offering to make entering the market worthwhile; *customer acceptability*, which means that your programs and services will be welcomed and accepted by customers; *ease of market entry*, which refers to your ability and that of competitors to enter a given market segment easily and the *number of existing competitors*, which determines if the market segment can support another provider. These secondary characteristics, when combined with the primary methods of market segmentation, add to the complexity of correctly determining a target market.

MARKET POSITIONING

Once you have segmented your market, you are ready to position yourself within that market. Market position, by definition, is the customer's perception of the place a small business occupies within a given market.

Small business owners may position their businesses according to the four P's of the marketing mix: **P**roduct, **P**rice, **P**lace and **P**romotion. Businesses may also position themselves according to the attributes and benefits of their programs and services or the price and quality of programs or services. More often than not, price reflects quality.

Another way to position a business is to be extremely customer service-oriented. Go out of your way to help customers. They will position your business for you. Other methods of positioning include targeting a specific user group, comparing one small business owner's services to another or using a combination of any of these methods. The ultimate purpose of market positioning is to create a perception in the minds of the customers that they must purchase your products, programs or services to satisfy their needs and desires.

ASK YOURSELF

► If you have never written a marketing plan, describe what you do use to guide your business.

► Review the contents of short, informal marketing plans. For each section, write down at least one idea or comment about your business. This will serve as the basis for your formal marketing plan.

► List the characteristics of your current customers and your ideal customer. What are you doing in your marketing to attract these ideal customers?

CHAPTER
FOURTEEN

DEVELOPING MARKETING STRATEGIES AND TACTICS

STRATEGIC ANALYSIS

The strategic analysis section of the marketing plan involves developing business goals and objectives, identifying opportunities for success and specifying strategies, tactics and action plans that must be implemented to achieve the desired results. Pay careful attention to the action plans that will be developed so you can maximize marketing potential with a minimum of risk.

This means you must specify completely the entire action plan, spelling out in detail each step to be taken. Communicate the action plan clearly to everyone who will be involved in marketing it successfully. This includes your staff, your marketing and sales reps, yourself—and your family, since they will probably talk about your business during the course of their normal day.

The components of the strategic analysis are:

Goals and Objectives—Properly develop and describe the goals and objectives for the business. Consider goals as achievements over the long term, such as a 10% increase in customer flow in one year. Objectives are the shorter-term levels of performance you need to achieve to reach your goals. An objective for the above goal might be to increase customer traffic by at least 2% per month, through a variety of marketing promotions targeted at current customers. This objective tells you not only *what* you will do, but *how* you will do it, and to *whom*. It specifies your behavior exactly. Write goal statements that are:

1. Specific to a particular activity

2. Measurable

3. Personal, related specifically to the business

4. Set within a reasonable time frame

5. Somewhat difficult, but not impossible, to achieve

6. Made known to an outside party so that you maintain your commitment to them

7. Objective and quantifiable, so you can measure your performance outcomes against the goal standard you set.

Your Turn — *Use the* Marketing Action Plan *(MAP) that follows to map every action plan you want to implement. It will help you achieve your business goals and objectives and will lead ultimately to your success.*

Marketing Action Plan

Goal:

Objective:

Actions:

Leader:

Strategies and Tactics—Strategies are the conceptual procedures by which the action plans will be organized to enable your business to achieve its goals and objectives. Strategies are very closely related to tactics, the methods by which the strategies are implemented. On your M.A.P. chart, your goals and objectives would determine your strategies, while the actions would be your tactics. An example of a strategy would be to create a communication program to inform residents within a five-mile radius of your store that you have opened a dry cleaning business in their neighborhood. The tactic would be to develop a direct mail campaign, obtain the mailing list, send out the direct mail piece and follow up with telephone calls.

The best way to understand strategies and tactics is that a strategy is the thought or decision-making process about what should be done and how it should be done, while a tactic is the actual implementation of that thought process.

Strategic Operating Assumptions—These are the expected external conditions under which your small business will operate. Identify the conditions most important to your small business, along with the trends that will occur during the time frame of the marketing plan. To determine the operating assumptions of a business, categorize them as economical (overall growth, inflation price trends, service costs), industry-related (business growth rates, new programs and service development, changes in service distribution patterns, changes in customer behavior and needs, changes in competitor's behavior) and outside influences (regulatory agencies, suppliers and vendors). Specify any other assumptions that may also be relevant to the business you can address them during the marketing campaign.

Strategic Opportunities—These are the opportunities that your business will expand upon to utilize its strengths best to improve its market position. You should have already identified most of these in your SWOT analysis. These opportunities can be other small business owners closing down their businesses, not having any competition in your geographic location or within your field or simply pricing your services so that the customer population can afford them—this also means using financing and credit cards, not necessarily discount pricing.

Strategic Obstacles—You should have gathered these in the *Threats* portion of your SWOT analysis. These strategic obstacles are the problems that currently exist that you must overcome to develop and maintain a successful small business. Some of these obstacles may take years to overcome, but you must be constantly aware of them and always be working on a solution for them.

One major mistake small business owners make is to think that problems, such as competition, will just go away. That is clearly not the case; research shows that competition in all aspects of the small business arena will increase over the next several years. This alone, then, is a strong argument for an appropriate marketing program. Again, you need to market your small business in order to be successful and profitable.

MARKETING MIX

Your final step in the development of the marketing portion of a comprehensive small business marketing plan is to determine your marketing mix. The marketing mix combines several integral elements to achieve recognition in the marketplace, a greater market share, a strong competitive position and a positive image with customers and colleagues. The goal of the marketing mix is to increase customer flow and sales.

The standard marketing mix consists of the four Ps of marketing:

▶ *Product (or Service)*—the products, programs and services you offer to customers who will purchase them for an agreed-upon price because they satisfy certain needs.

▶ *Price*—what the customer will pay for your products, programs and services—a function of perceived value. If the customer perceives the quality and value of what you sell to be high, there will be no argument over your price.

► *Place*—how and where you will distribute products and services to your customer. The place can be the customer's office, your office or store or any other location that will serve the purpose. Place also includes direct mail, warehouses and personal delivery.

► *Promotion*—the series of communications you use to inform customers and referral sources of your products and services and their need-satisfying capabilities. Communications methods include advertising, publicity, public relations, personal sales and sales promotion. These methods will be described in more detail later in this chapter.

These four Ps are the basic components of every marketing mix. They are completely synergistic, with the total effect of a good mix greater than the sum of its parts. No single component can ever stand alone; for the marketing mix to be effective, each must be developed in conjunction with the others.

Four other components must now be added to the basic marketing mix. These additional four Ps include *Positioning,* the perception customers have of your business based on its unique and different qualities; *People,* the employees in your office or store and how they interact with the customers as well as to the customers; *Politics,* any laws and other regulations that govern the conduct of your business; and *Profit,* what you expect to make as a result of your marketing plan.

Service is the one final element. Never omit service from your marketing mix. How will you service your customers? How will you handle their telephone calls, problems, complaints? How much training in customer relations will you give your staff? And, what will you do to be proactive in your customer service and marketing-related service efforts?

You must consider these basic service factors to market a successful small business, especially if you expect your customers to buy from you again and to provide you with referrals.

Be aware that everything in the marketing mix and the strategies and tactics for the marketing plan focus on satisfying the needs of your customers. In turn, your needs are satisfied as you operate a customer-centered, profit-making business. Therefore, your obvious goal in developing a proper marketing mix is to increase customer traffic, sales and satisfaction.

Your Turn　　**The techniques for developing a basic marketing mix for a small business are presented in the form on pages 271 and 272, Developing the Marketing Mix. Fill in the spaces and you will have the information you need to conduct your marketing program.**

Remember that there are times when too much planning and analysis can lead to paralysis. Certain situations require that you act quickly without extensive planning. Failure to do so will result in another small business owner securing a customer whom you might have had.

If you do all your initial planning and marketing development early on in your business and remain flexible enough to revise it as conditions warrant, you will be able to develop a situation-specific marketing mix as the need arises. The result will be an effective execution and implementation of your strategies and tactics, which will lead to a successful operation of your small business.

PROMOTIONAL MIX

In this last section of the marketing plan, you describe in detail everything you will do to communicate with customers. These communication techniques will activate the strategies and tactics and bring in customers.

Advertising is paid-for media communications small business owners use to inform customers that products, services and programs are available. *Sales promotions* include a variety of techniques that introduce customers to a service and motivate

Developing the Marketing Mix

What does the company want to achieve this year?

_____

How much money do we want to make? What is our desired profit margin?

_____

Where is the industry in the product life cycle and what strategies are necessary to compete in this pase?

_____

Who is our target market and what is our unique position in their minds?

_____

What is our time frame for achieving our business and financial goals?

_____

What resources do we have to implement the necessary tactics to achieve the strategies we develop in the marketing mix?

_____

Are there any specific legal ramifications or requirements related to our product or service?

_____

Do we have the required licenses, patents, trademarks and registrations for our product or service?

_____

Does our product or service infringe on any trademarked or registered product or service? If so, how will we overcome this obstacle?

_____

Developing the Marketing Mix (continued)

1. Target market selection/market segmentation characteristics:

2. Products/programs/services offered:

Name: _____

| **Features** | **Benefits** | **Need satisfaction** |

3. Distribution channels (accessibility and availability):

4. Price (includes discounts, incentives and payment terms):

5. Promotions:
   A. Types of communications:

   B. Techniques
      1. Advertising
      2. Publicity
      3. Public relations
      4. Business publications: brochures, flyers
      5. Direct mail
      6. Personal selling
      7. Telemarketing
      8. Networking
      9. Speeches
     10. Community service

Follow the form above to develop your own marketing mix.

Fill in one sheet for each product or service you offer. Every product or service or every different market you serve should have its own marketing mix.

them to buy, usually at a discounted rate. *Personal sales* involve direct contact between small business owners or their representatives and potential customers. *Publicity* refers to free media placements of information about a small business, its programs and services and even its personnel. In contrast, *public relations* involves activities and efforts that will cause the community to view the small business owner and the entire small business in a positive manner.

The promotional mix combines these five elements to create awareness of your products, programs and services; to induce customers to try them and to influence customers to buy from you again.

The success of the mix is totally dependent on the quality and perceived value of what you are offering for sale, the readiness of the customer to buy or use what you are selling and the methods of communication used to inform the customers of the availability of your service.

Advertising

Advertising is any paid form of presentation of a small business owner's ideas. It is impersonal because there is no direct person-to-person contact. Advertising is done through newspapers, radio, television, magazines, brochures, fliers, forms, displays and third party word-of-mouth. All these methods present your message, but there is no way to totally measure their impact or effect; you cannot always determine if a customer came to you as a result of a single advertising campaign or some other influence, or a combination of influences. Of course, most small business owners would like to believe that increased customer flow should be due solely to the advertising effort, but that is not always the case. Increased customer flow often results from other promotional techniques or from personal referrals. Whatever the case may be, a business tries to fulfill one or several objectives with its advertising campaign.

The first objective is to publicize products and services. The goal is to inform prospective customers of the many ways your small business can satisfy their needs. This objective can be met by advertising one product, program or service or by advertising the entire sales line.

The second objective of an advertising campaign is to increase the demand for your product, program or service to increase customer traffic. You may also want to consider an increase in prices, based on the results and effectiveness of your advertising. Through your advertising, you are also trying to get customers of your competitors to transfer their loyalty to your business.

By meeting this second advertising objective, you will naturally meet the third objective: to create a recognizable name and a positive image of the business. Since this is an objective of public relations, in addition to advertising, the advertising and public relations efforts would support each other.

An advertising program may try to achieve several other objectives, such as public information or employee motivation. Also, small business owners must understand the difference between product advertising and service advertising.

Product Advertising

Product advertising is very simple: a company has a tangible product they wish to inform the public about. They develop advertisements to communicate this information. They even show a picture of the product in the ad. Pick up any trade journal in any industry and look at all the product advertising. You will see ads for a variety of technical products to help you run your business more efficiently and to help customers run their lives more effectively. This is product advertising.

Service Advertising

Service advertising is more difficult. Ads cannot show service in action. This makes it very difficult to identify distinctions between small business owners, especially small business owners in the same field. The following suggestions will help you differentiate your small business' services from those of your competitors and inform the public of what you have to offer.

1. Develop the ad in terms of the customer's needs, not the needs of the business

2. Make certain each ad addresses only one service at a time

3. Target the ads to your geographical service area

4. Define the service as if you were the first small business owner to offer it

5. Place the ads on a regular basis

6. Be totally honest and open in describing the products, programs and services you are offering to the public

7. Make sure all your ads, even for services, are direct response.

The small business owner that follows these rules will achieve a measurable level of success. However, most small business owners do not possess the in-house capabilities to generate professional and attention-getting ads. They must hire an outside advertising agency.

I hope you fired your ad agency. However, if you *must* work with an ad agency, follow these guidelines to determine if they can do the job for you.

► Identify the skills of the agency's personnel

► Ensure their understanding of your products, programs and services and what you are trying to do with them

► Determine their ability to provide all the services that your company may need, such as ad production, copy writing, placements, market research and creative work

► Request references about their work with other small business owners

► Identify any conflicts of interest with other accounts

► Determine their ability to meet deadlines

► Identify their procedure for tracking the impact and results of the advertising campaign

► Make sure they communicate clearly their methods for charging and billing for their work and arranging their payment terms

► Clarify their techniques for reporting information to you

► Finally, interview the agency and make sure you are satisfied that their representatives interact well with you and your staff.

Media Selection

Determining the method through which the information about your business is communicated to the public is media selection. The most common media are television, radio, newspapers, magazines, brochures, fliers, billboards, direct mail and word-of-mouth. Most small business owners think in terms of placing their ads in the three main media: television, radio and print—usually newspaper or magazine.

Cover the following when you discuss advertising media selection in your marketing plan:

► **Selectivity** is the medium's ability to reach a specific geographic segment or target market—selected customers. Many small business owners choose to advertise in a special section of a trade journal or newspaper, since this section is usually targeted for their business and industry.

► **Penetration** is the extent to which the medium actually reaches the target market. Your media rep can tell you how many people, on average, will see or hear your ad. You can determine the effectiveness of the placements by tracking the responses to the advertisement and developing a percentage rating of the actual responses to the quoted penetration.

► **Coverage** is the percentage of the total market a medium is able to reach. If your ad appears in a regional issue of the newspaper, it should reach 100% of the readership in that area. However, if it is placed in the entire paper, not everyone may see your ad.

► **Flexibility** of a medium is determined by how far in advance an advertising commitment must be made. Newspapers and radio are usually more flexible than television, and local newspapers and magazines are more flexible than major papers.

► **Cost** is usually the single most important determinant of which advertising medium will be selected. There are times when the cost of advertising with a particular medium is so prohibitive, such as television during the Super Bowl game, that a small business owner cannot afford to buy the space or time. Then, you will want to select a less expensive medium, one that meets the other criteria in accordance with the marketing objectives of your company. Most small business owners tend to purchase print space, since that seems to be the most cost effective for them. You may want to consider the cost of using smaller print ads, supplementing them with radio advertisements.

► **Editorial Environment** determines the tone or the setting in which the advertisement appears, which influences how it is perceived by the target audience. Media with high audience acceptance and perceived credibility should be strongly considered for advertising placements. Customers will associate their positive perceptions of a particular medium with the programs or services that are advertised in it.

Consider these categories when you discuss advertising in your marketing plan. List information for each, so that you and anyone else can go back and check whether your advertising adheres to your original plan requirements. If not, either change your plan to meet current needs or, if your plan requirements are still valid, revise your advertising.

I must include a word of caution here, because I have seen too many small businesses get caught up in what they think advertising can do for them. Never enter an advertising campaign with lofty ideals of what will be accomplished. Advertising can and cannot do certain things for your small business.

1. Advertising gives your company the opportunity to say what it wants, but this medium lacks full credibility because the consumer knows the space and time were purchased

2. Advertising can inform the public about your products, programs and services

3. Advertising can help create name recognition, a positive image and a good reputation for the small business owner

4. All advertising must be direct response to generate some form of action on the part of the customer through its persuasive and needs-satisfying messages

5. Advertising cannot work on its own, without an overall marketing plan; because of the impersonal nature of advertising, it cannot bring a customer into the office or store

6. Finally, advertising can help your small business support its market position and increase its market penetration.

No matter how you choose to advertise or which agency you choose to work with, the advertising campaign will be based on the Four Ms of advertising. *Media* refers to the method you use to get your message across. The *message* is what you are trying to say. The *market* is the people you are trying to reach with your message. *Money* refers to the cost of the advertising campaign. These four Ms will always determine the extent of every small business owner's advertising program. Make sure you describe them in detail and discuss their relationship in your marketing plan.

Remember that, to be effective, advertising programs must be supported by a variety of other promotional techniques. The final result of a good marketing and advertising campaign is a new customer. You can always judge success by how many customers come into your office or store to buy from you.

Sales Promotions: Objectives and Timing

Promotions are nonpersonal communications that supplement and complement advertising and personal selling and make them both more effective. Promotions are similar to advertising; they attempt to communicate information to potential customers about the need-satisfying capabilities of a product, program or service. Promotions are not paid placements in another medium. Rather, they are most often small business owner-sponsored programs designed to influence customers to purchase now by offering some type of incentive. The incentive can be a free trial of something, a discount or a multiple purchase at a reduced price. Include an expiration date on all sales promotions to motivate the customer to receive the perceived financial or personal gain by being involved before the promotion ends.

Common objectives for any sales promotion campaign include stimulating an immediate increase in customer flow and revenue, creating a sense of urgency among potential customers to come in for products and services, encouraging customers to buy more of the service than they would have normally bought and producing excitement among customers because you have something new and/or of value for them to purchase. Effective use of sales promotions must be maintained within the ethical code of conduct for small business owners, the constraints of the overall marketing plan and within the budgetary guidelines established for promotional activities.

Sales promotions can be very beneficial to your small business. However, it is important for small business owners to remember that they must not oversaturate the marketplace with constant sales promotions. Continuous promotions will be perceived by customers as a ploy to get them to use products and services that are not needed. Effective sales promotions must be used strategically or they will not increase consumer demand for those products and services. Strategically timed promotions convince customers, both new and repeat, to try the programs and services you offer. This is especially true if the promotion is a discounted price for something you are selling. People have a tendency to repurchase previously tried products and services or to try new ones when there is little or no financial risk involved.

Publicity

Many of the methods used to promote your small business will involve publicity. Publicity is communication designed to influence consumer buying behavior, just like advertising. However, publicity is not sponsored by the company, nor is it necessarily designed to stimulate sales. Theoretically, it is free.

Publicity involves media exposure for your small business that is basically nonsponsored and unpaid advertising. The major goal of any publicity campaign is to increase the name recognition, reputation and credibility of the small business owner and, along with public relations, create a favorable and positive image.

Many methods through which a small business owner can receive publicity are covered in greater detail throughout this book. They are mentioned here so that you can list them in your written marketing plan; use the detailed information in other chapters to make the plans work.

If you are viewed as a reliable resource for information in your field, newspaper, television and radio reporters will seek you out to help with a story. You might be viewed as the authoritative source on a subject, possessing so much credibility that the media chooses to produce a story about your small business. A small business owner may be offering a new type of service or an old service with a new twist that a broadcast medium may think is newsworthy. And, small business owners can send news releases or hold press conferences announcing major events.

Remember to consider the other publicity methods that were also discussed in more detail in other parts of the book.

You can write an article for a newspaper, magazine or professional journal; give free speeches and seminars; work with charity organizations; be a guest on radio and television shows; attend local business group and professional meetings and network. Whatever method you choose, the idea remains the same: Get someone else to tell your customers about your business without your having to pay for it.

Publicity is like any other portion of the promotional mix. Think of it as an integral part of your overall marketing program, and use it strategically. If you think that everything that occurs within your business is worth free publicity and you inform the media accordingly, the media will begin to view your business as extremely self-serving. Then when you really do have something newsworthy to offer to customers, the media will not provide publicity for fear it is just another unwarranted request. Therefore, plan your publicity campaign carefully, and use the various methods judiciously to maintain your position as a credible source of small business information. Then make certain you use good public relations to augment your publicity campaign.

Public Relations

The primary goal of public relations (PR) is to foster a positive image of your small business in the minds of customers. Although that definition seems simple enough, public relations is probably the most misunderstood concept in the entire promotional mix.

Public relations has been confused with advertising, which it is not, and with publicity, which it may result in, result from or lead to, at one time or another. Public relations involves various forms of communications that cost your business financially in a manner different from advertising or sales promotions. Consider costs such as personal salaries, planning time, program development and program implementation, as well as office supplies, telephone, travel and other business-related expenses. Many of these expenses are intangible. Too often, they are forgotten in the marketing plan budget.

It is imperative to make money available for public relations in the same way that monies are allocated for advertising and sales promotions. Include a public relations budget in your marketing plan, along with a public relations schedule. Both can be included in larger sections. The PR budget can be part of the overall marketing budget and the PR schedule can be part of the advertising/media schedule. Just make certain that items allocated and related to PR are clearly identified in your marketing plan.

Design your small business's public relations program to create a positive image of you, as owner, and the business in the minds of the customers. Since many small business owners offer similar programs and services, it is important that you differentiate your public relations effort by informing customers of your uniqueness in serving them, your high quality products, programs and services, and your constant customer contact and service. This last point is extremely important, especially since repeat business is usually a function of how well customers are treated throughout the course of their relationship with you.

A successful public relations program will be based on the following criteria. It:

1. Exposes and projects the small business owner's greatest strengths and capabilities to the community in general and to the target market in particular.

2. Emphasizes your expertise in your field, as well as the quality of service you give to customers.

3. Competes successfully with the public relations efforts of your competitors.

4. Allows for measurement and evaluation of the information it provides to the target audience and to other prospective customers.

5. Is done in-house or, if you use an outside agency, the program remains internally driven. Quite often, cost and availability of internal staff determine whether or not a small business runs its own campaign.

6. Creates and maintains the desired image for the small business owner within the community with customers and with other small business owners.

7. Supports and enhances all other aspects of the marketing program.

When you write this section of your marketing plan, make certain your public relations program meets all these criteria. If it does not, list the criteria the program does not meet. Identify what you will do to improve the program so those criteria are quickly met. Remember, the more you specify in your marketing plan *before* you implement, the easier it will be to implement.

The value of a good promotional program in general and a good public relations campaign in particular is seen in the results. Program effectiveness is determined by heightened community awareness about your small business, the products and services you offer, increased customer flow, establishment of you as the primary source and resource for business information, enhanced community good-will, a respected and credible reputation and the development of an expanded referral base. These results can also be achieved through an informal public relations effort, simply by having your staff be very personable and service-oriented to everyone they meet. The personal touch, which is lacking from advertising and sales promotions, vastly improves a formal public relations campaign and supports the advertising program.

In your marketing plan describe the personal service and public relations responsibilities of your staff. Let them read it in the plan. When they see it, they will know you are serious about using this approach as a marketing tool.

One final comment must be made regarding public relations. Everything a small business owner does should be considered public relations. Contacts with customers, other small business owners, staff members of another business, the general public, and the provision of your products, programs and services are more obvious, and perhaps more tangible, methods of public relations. However, less obvious techniques are also powerful customer influences. These include the office decor, stationary, staff dress, time spent with each customer, amount of time a customer has to wait to receive services or to be approached by a salesperson, telephone manners of the staff, their manners of speech and body language. If there is an uncertainty about how to deal with these items, remember to keep everything professional, positive, upbeat and friendly. The desired results will come naturally. Again, when you write your marketing plan, I strongly recommend you specify how each of these items will be carried out.

Personal Selling

It is imperative that you sell. Everyone sells all the time. Train your staff in how to sell your products, programs or services. Describe the training programs you will provide. If you create your own sales training manual, consider including it as an addendum to the marketing plan. If you are going to send your people to seminars, specify what seminars they will attend.

Then, have them read Chapter 10 in this book. It describes the basics of selling that everyone, from the new salesperson to the seasoned veteran, must go through. There is also information on some advanced sales skills that can increase sales rates by more than 100%.

Use your personal background and experience to help your people become better sales professionals. You have probably encountered many objections related to your business when you try to sell someone. Write them into the marketing plan, along with a description of how you handle each objection. Make this part of everyone's training.

Again, the more you include up front in the marketing plan, the easier it will be to implement every aspect of the plan.

Marketing Results and Support Documents

The last two sections of the marketing plan are often left out. Include them, as they will help you successfully implement your plan.

The *marketing results* section describes the results you expect from your efforts. These can be in financial terms, number of customers, return on investment, percentage increases in customers, revenues and profits or anything else you think of to describe your desired results clearly.

Support documents include any and all legal contracts, sample ads, sample press releases, media schedules, forms and charts, budgets and pro formas, and other material that supports or enhances your marketing plan.

CHAPTER SUMMARY

The last two chapters provided an overview of how to write a marketing plan. Several important questions must be answered prior to developing and implementing your marketing plan. These include, What is the nature and mission of your small business? Who are the customers and competitors? What are the financial requirements of the business? How and when will products and services be distributed? What is the preferred image for the business? Once these questions have been answered to your satisfaction, use them as the basis for a more in-depth analysis of your entire marketing program.

The marketing program consists of several activities that precede implementation of the plan and several that serve as the action part of the plan. The precursors include a market analysis, market research, strategic analysis, the identification of particular programs and services that will be offered to selected market segments and the development of the marketing mix. The marketing mix contains the product or service you will provide, its price structures, how it will be distributed to customers and the type of advertising and promotions that will make customers want to come see you.

The *marketing mix* is the key to an effective marketing program. It must be activated through a variety of tactical and promotional techniques. These include advertising, public relations, personal sales and sales promotions, which usually refer to discounted services or other incentives. Other tactics relate to how well you treat your customer during his or her visit and the type of follow-up service that is provided after and between purchases. All of these will influence whether or not a customer starts or continues to buy from you.

Marketing a small business is relatively new for most small business owners. It is unrealistic to think that everyone possesses the expertise to do so. Most small business owners are experts at what they do. However, more often than not, small business owners do not have the skills and capabilities to be professional marketers, nor do they have the time.

If you do not have the time to write your own marketing plan—either an informal one or a formal, comprehensive plan—seek outside professional marketing help. Your investment will be well worth your return. The greatest number of small business failures are due not to poor knowledge or undercapitalization or service on the part of small business owners, but to inadequate marketing. Remember, to be successful you must develop your marketing plan to help you market, market, market.

ASK YOURSELF

► Have you written a comprehensive marketing plan? Discuss why you do or do not use it.

► Assume you have a promotional mix budget. What is your best application of this money at this time? Describe in detail how you will promote your business and what you are willing to spend on each tactic.

► Write your marketing plan. Then, create a goal log that you fill in every time you look at the plan. Also, create a results log to determine the effectiveness of your marketing campaigns. Do you see any similarities between the two logs? Do your results improve every time you review and implement the ideas in your marketing plan?

APPENDIXES

Appendix I
Direct Mail

Advantages of Direct Mail

- ► Quicker and easier to produce than traditional advertising

- ► Testing is quicker and easier, especially with a small area

- ► Response is quicker, so tracking for effectiveness happens sooner

- ► Can be cheaper than traditional advertising, especially when used for a small test market

- ► Highly targeted, and can reach hard-to-reach customers

- ► Greater flexibility to change what is not working

- ► Longer copy can provide more information and details

- ► Can make more descriptive and multiple offers

- ► Easy for customers to respond to

- ► Helps build a prospect and customer list

Ten Ways To Use Direct Mail

1. Lead generation; get inquiries; build a mailing list.

2. Supplement or boost sales.

3. Offer free trials or samples.

4. Inform customers about special sales or private sales.

5. Conduct surveys and other types of research.

6. Publicize your product, program or service.

7. Keep in touch with key customers.

8. Sell licensing rights to users of your product or service.

9. Create other distribution channels.

10. Make direct sales.

Additional Ways to Improve Your Direct Mail Offer and Your Response Rates

1. Place a time limit or expiration date on your offer.

2. Offer a premium or a special report with a purchase.

3. Offer a free trial period, like the book and record clubs provide. Give customers 15, 30 or 60 days to try out your product.

4. Offer several different versions of your product or service, at different price points.

5. Provide a sample or a demonstration version of your product or service.

6. Offer a discount or other type of believable, special offer.

7. Unconditionally guarantee customer satisfaction. Reverse the risk totally so the customer is in a complete win-win situation.

8. Double the guarantee by giving them a premium they can keep, even if they return the product.

9. Pay for postage, both on delivery and returns.

10. Offer a contest or a sweepstakes with a high perceived value prize. Use involvement devices such as rub-offs, fill-ins or tear-offs.

11. Offer payment terms for every purchase, including credit cards, 0% interest for a specified time, and no payments for 90 days.

12. Use toll-free telephone numbers and fax numbers to speed up responses.

13. Use a business reply card if confidential information is not required.

14. Use an order form and an envelope if confidential information is required.

15. Send $1 with your offer to get them to respond.

How to Improve Your Direct Mail Sales Letters

▶ Speak and write directly to one person

▶ Sell benefits first, middle and last

▶ Give them an immediate reason—major benefit—to keep reading

▶ Ask for the order several times

▶ Provide a call to action and tell the reader how to use it

▶ Make your point

▶ Use key words such as *you, your, yours, new, free, bonus, success* and *satisfaction guaranteed*

▶ Provide testimonials

▶ Write as much interesting copy as you have to, to inform the customer about your product or service and to make the sale

▶ Offer free information, whether they buy now or not

▶ Give them an alternative response in addition to *yes* or *no*

▶ Remain personal and personable throughout the letter

▶ Be honest and truthful with everything you write

▶ Give them a reason to do business with you

▶ Use a *P.S.* at the end of your letter

▶ Use involvement devices, such as scratch-off tickets, pull tabs or stamps

▶ End each page with an incomplete sentence, so the reader must continue on to the next page

▶ Use short sentences and short paragraphs

▶ Use a Johnson box: a box of asterisks at the top of the page

Ten Ways To Improve Your Direct Mail Response Forms

1. First and foremost, make it look like an order form.

2. Make the order form easy for the reader to find. Keep it simple. Give them enough room to write their information on it.

3. Limit their choices to no more than two or three items. Any more confuses the reader.

4. Repeat the offer on the response form that you made in the sales letter.

5. Print your satisfaction guarantee on the response or order form.

6. Code your response forms so you can track their effectiveness.

7. Include two types of response forms, such as an envelope and a reply card. This increases the probability they will respond.

8. If possible, write the prospect or customer's name on the order form.

9. If you can, offer a toll-free telephone ordering option. Also, if you can, accept credit cards.

10. Offer to send the product C.O.D. You will increase your response rate dramatically. Even if 50% of the people to whom you ship the product eventually refuse it, you are still ahead, because more people responded to your offer.

Appendix II
Advertising Techniques

Suggestions for Improving Your Advertising Techniques

1. Position your products, programs or services so the customer identifies them with your business name.

2. Your advertising budget should be designed according to how much is necessary to reach a specific revenue objective. I do not recommend using percentage of sales to determine the advertising budget; advertising is supposed to produce sales, not vice versa. Determine—through research, trial and error, and sometimes, just plain luck—what it should cost to inform the public of your products and services so that a certain dollar amount of revenue will be generated.

3. There are times when competitors' ads should be presented to customers first. Their opinions will identify the strengths and weaknesses of your competitors so you can develop ads that will more appropriately appeal to your target customer group. The easiest way to do this is to walk up to people and ask them what they think about an ad. Get them to spell out their likes and dislikes. Then, you can create a better ad because you have more information about what the customer wants and needs.

4. The headline of an ad is extremely important. It must scream a benefit and get the reader involved. Begin the headline with "Which . . ." It is almost impossible to write a bad headline or ad when it begins with "Which . . ." Never start an ad with a headline that asks for a yes or no answer to a question; if the customer/reader answers no, you have lost them. Also, give them choices in the headline, so that either response will be positive.

5. The most important information conveyed to the customer must be in the headline, such as helping a customer satisfy a need or solve a problem. The remainder of the ad must be written so that it is closely tied to the headline. You may not believe that people will take the time to read the copy of an ad, but once they are interested in the headline, they will read through the copy, especially if they feel the ad addresses them personally. Furthermore, people will read a long-copy ad more often than they will read a short-copy one, especially when the copy is interesting and motivating.

6. Write ads so they are directed toward prime customers. Close every ad with a phrase or slogan they will remember and a call to action. This helps them identify your business as being unique and different from your competitors.

7. Keep print ad sizes down. Supplement them and expand the audience with radio spots every so often. Choose these situations carefully, based on your marketing objectives and budget.

8. Tell people what they want to hear, but do not make any claims about programs or services that cannot be substantiated. Tell them how you can help them achieve their goals, but be honest, sincere and professional, and have support for your statements. Remember, when you make any statement of fact, you must have proof.

9. Be ready to alter ads as the audience or media tools change. You may have had early success with newspaper ads, but now have to modify your approach because you do not seem to be reaching your audience. You might go to a direct mail piece, a letter or a brochure sent to potential customers. This ensures that they get your information and become aware of your products and services. Another suggestion is to place an ad in a professional or trade journal, if you work business-to-business. While this ad may not immediately bring you customers, it surely will be seen by other noncompeting small business owners who may refer customers to you.

10. Evaluate your advertising program periodically and make adjustments where necessary. Advertising is a campaign, a series of ads, not just a one-time thing. The ads must change as the audience or your message changes. Test everything, and make changes according to your test results.

Remember,

ALL ADVERTISING MUST BE DIRECT RESPONSE.

Appendix III
Sales

The Sales Presentation

Here are several ideas to help you develop a more effective sales presentation. It goes without saying that you must first know your product, service or whatever you are trying to sell. Then be prepared to make the sale. Your presentation should include material that relates to the following acronym:

A = **Attention.** Get your prospect's undivided attention before you continue with your presentation.

I = **Interest.** Arouse their interest in what you are attempting to sell.

D = **Desire.** Your presentation should either create or further their desire to purchase your product or service.

A = **Action.** Move them to action, which means closing the sale.

Another approach that will improve your sales presentation is to use a client-centered orientation, rather than a product orientation. The typical sales presentation will focus on what is being sold. This includes detailed descriptions of features, attributes and anything else related to the product. Their goal is to focus on the salesperson's needs. A client-centered sales presentation focuses on the customer's needs, wants, and desires. You present the benefits the client will receive from purchasing your product or service. You discuss how your product or service will solve any problems the client may have or satisfy any unmet needs. Then the client will want to buy from you and become your customer.

The Sales Plan

The sales plan is actually a microcosm of the larger marketing plan. The sales plan specifies the actions that will be taken for each customer, to make the sale and achieve the marketing goals. The sales plan includes the following:

1. Identify specific prospects.

2. Prioritize them according to their potential to become customers. You will contact the primary prospects first.

3. Develop a customer profile and a customer conversion procedure for each prospect.

4. Prepare your selling message and presentation.

5. Try to anticipate objections and your responses.

6. Project the drop out rate for each step of the sales process.

7. Forecast how many prospects you must contact to achieve your sales goals and objectives.

Ten Steps to Successful Selling

Selling is a set of skills that can and must be learned to be successful in any endeavor. The successful salesperson is a combination of friend, counselor, marketer, product manager and all-around nice person. These are the qualities that help make a sale. In fact, many purchases are made simply because the buyer liked one salesperson more than another, all other things being equal. To be a successful salesperson, learn to develop these skills:

1. **Be Prepared**—Know yourself, your product or service, your price structure, and rehearse your presentation.

2. **Know Your Customers**—Find out and understand their needs, wants and desires, who your competition is for their business and who the other purchasing influences are.

3. **Read the Walls**—Look at what your customer has on the walls and in his or her office. This will inform you about his or her personality, likes and dislikes.

4. **Establish a Relationship**—This means make certain the situation is comfortable. Let the customer speak, while you listen and provide advice at the appropriate times.

5. **Practice Keeping Quiet**—Speak in short, clear, concise sentences to make your points, then keep quiet. Practice the *Golden Minute of Silence,* to let your customer speak.

6. **Use Open-Ended Questions**—More than simple yes/no questions, this involves your customer. It also allows you to maintain control of the presentation.

7. **Anticipate Objections**—This should be done during your rehearsal, but whenever you do it, resolve them before they are even voiced. State new and restate already-mentioned benefits.

8. **Turn Objections into Information Requests**—This is all objections really are anyway. Customers are asking you to provide more information as to why they should buy from you.

9. **Watch for Closing Signals**—These can be words, gestures, eye movements, requests for more information about the product or service, or a return to previous points.

10. **Ask for the Check**—To get their business, ask for their business.

How To Handle Objections

Every salesperson encounters numerous objections during his or her career. Rather than try to list all the objections here and provide responses for them, I will describe a simple, seven-step system that can be applied to any situation. All you have to do is practice with the system so that it is activated automatically during your sales presentation. You should then be able to handle any objection.

1. Listen to the *entire* objection. Do not interrupt the prospect with your response. If you let them talk, they will often answer their own objection.

2. Feed the objection back. When you repeat the objection to the prospect, they will usually elaborate on it and answer their own objection.

3. Ask them directly to elaborate on the objection. As the prospect responds, listen for information that you can use to handle the objection or that you can feed back to the prospect so he or she will answer the objection.

4. Answer the objection. Do this honestly, even if you must admit that your product or service has a few weaknesses. Never get flustered or argue with the prospect. Remember that an objection is another way of asking for more information.

5. Confirm the answer. Once the objection has been answered, repeat the answer verbatim, and ask the prospect to agree with you.

6. Move on. When the objection has been answered, move on to the next part of your presentation. You may want to use a transitional statement such as "By the way . . .", and then continue with the presentation.

7. Close the sale. There are many situations when the best time to close is right after handling an objection. Watch for your prospect's responses and buying signals.

The Anatomy of a Close

Closing a sale is really as simple as ABC—you should Always Be Closing. If you break down the close into its component parts, you will find that closing a sale is really much easier than most people believe.

1. **Know your prospects.** Understand their wants, needs, desires and how you can help them solve their problems. Understand their buying habits and motives.

2. **Recognize their buying signals.** Be aware of the verbal and visual cues they provide, such as asking you to repeat a previous portion of the presentation or asking more questions.

3. **Make their decision to buy.** Decide that the best thing for your prospect is to buy what you are selling. Lead them to making the buying decision on their own.

4. **Be confident when you close.** You must believe in yourself and in what you are selling. Begin to write the order casually; assume they are buying.

5. **Maintain your closing momentum.** Once you start to close, continue to close. Do not change directions and move on to something else. In fact, you may want to begin your presentation with a close. This will provide you with closing momentum throughout the entire meeting.

6. **Pause.** There are various times during your presentation when your prospect's attention may start to wander. Whenever you notice this happening, pause, look directly into your prospect's eyes and wait until you have his or her undivided attention.

7. **Be quiet.** Once you have asked for the order, remain silent. A cardinal rule of selling is, "He who speaks first, loses." Therefore, when you ask for the order or simply ask an important question during the presentation, be quiet and wait for the prospect to speak.

Developing Your Telemarketing Skills

There is a great deal of information available on how to speak to someone on the telephone. You are not involved in a hard-sell situation. Your prospects should already be pre-qualified as interested in purchasing what you are selling. Speak to them in a natural manner.

The best advice is to be yourself on the telephone. You may want to have an outline to guide you when you make your business calls, but the entire call does not have to be scripted. The things you must remember include:

1. Always be yourself when speaking on the telephone.

2. Always have a definite reason for calling.

3. Introduce yourself immediately when the other person answers.

4. Try to use the person's name three times in the first five to 10 seconds of the call. Everyone likes to hear their name mentioned.

5. Be confident about your call. You are a professional and an expert, and you have something very beneficial to offer.

6. Listen more than you speak. The prospect will tell you everything you want to know if you only give him or her the chance.

7. Compliment the prospect/customer whenever you can. Create a positive atmosphere for the telephone conversation.

8. Be polite and courteous. Remember, there is no hard sell. In fact, today's consumer is more educated than ever before and will be turned off quickly by a hard sell.

9. Briefly explain the purpose of your call, but not so quickly that your prospect has trouble understanding you. Then, listen to your prospect/customer. When you speak, try to ask open-ended questions so they continue to be involved in the conversation. Stay away from yes/no questions whenever possible.

10. Always try to close your sale. To make a sale, ask the prospect for an order. Always Be Closing. Many sales are lost because the salesperson neglected to close. If you think *Close* from the beginning, you will be more successful. Constantly remind the prospect of the benefits of your offer. More often than not, they will close themselves.

Cold Call Telemarketing Techniques

The cold call is the most difficult of all sales calls to make. It is more difficult on the telephone than in person, because the prospect can easily hang up the phone at any time during your presentation. Here are some tips and techniques to help you over the hurdles of cold call telemarketing:

1. Prepare your presentation before you call. It should not sound as if you are reading from a script, but you should have some type of script or outline available.

2. Try to learn something about your prospect *before* you call. This may require an information-gathering call at an earlier date or a conversation with someone who knows the prospect.

3. Take a deep breath and smile before you call. Prepare to speak in a positive, uplifting and confident voice.

4. Introduce yourself when the prospect answers by stating your name and your company's name. Try to say the prospect's name at least three times during the first five to 10 seconds of the call.

5. During your introduction, say something relevant to the prospect's needs.

6. Mention a benefit the prospect can readily understand.

7. Try to sell the appointment, not the product or service. You are trying to meet the prospect face-to-face, which should make your sales presentation easier. However, if the prospect can be sold over the telephone, close the sale.

8. Do not discuss price on the telephone. The prospect will try to talk about price, costs or discounts. You maintain that what you are selling has great value for the prospect and can provide substantial savings. You will be glad to discuss price in a personal meeting.

9. Confirm the appointment. Schedule it, get the prospect to repeat it and then you repeat it again.

10. Thank the prospect for the time spent on the telephone. Confirm the appointment time and date before you hang up.

Appendix IV
Perception

Sensory Perceptual Style Processor Equivalents

Every sensory perceptual style has its own language. The language of one style also has an equivalent in the other two styles. These are called processor equivalents. It is up to you, and necessary for your complete understanding of sensory perceptual styles, to identify these and other terms related to each particular style. For example, anything having to do with seeing or images is visual, hearing or sounds or speaking is auditory, and feeling or touch is kinesthetic. The list below provides you with some of these processor equivalents. Once you identify that the words someone is using belong to a specific sensory perceptual style, to achieve rapport you must personally match those words and that style. This may mean you have to change your sensory perceptual communication style for a particular situation, and that is exactly what you will do because you want to communicate successfully.

Visual	Auditory	Kinesthetic
See	Hear	Feel
Look	Listen	Touch
Bright	Loud	Pressing
Picture	Sound	Feeling
Colorful	Melodious	Exciting
Illuminate	Be Heard	Be Felt
Clear	Harmonious	Fits
Dawn	Tune In	Firm
Flash	Crescendo	Spike
Appear	Discuss	Aware
Perspective	Expression	Hands-on
Focused	Listen To	Secure
Foggy	Off-key	Clumsy
Strobe	Harsh	Irritate
Form	Resonance	Angle
Visual	Vocal	Do/Act
Imagine	Speak	Be
Perception	Attention	Action
Blank Out	Inner Voices	Fidget

Examples of Perceptual Language—Analogies

Kinesthetic	Visual	Auditory
I just feel that . . .	The way it looks to me . . .	I tell myself . . .
Let's get in touch.	See you soon.	Talk to you in a little while.
I can't get a handle on this at all.	Clearly, we have different perspectives.	You're talking out of both sides of your mouth.
struggle, smooth, comfort, grasp tight, out of touch	bright, clear, vague, focus, flash, colorful, dark, bright	harmonious, explain, orchestrate, tone, amplify, discuss
"You give me goose bumps."	"You light up my life."	"You ring my chimes."
still	dark	silent
roller coaster	disco light show	cacophony
crumbs in bed	messy room	fingernails on blackboard
get things straightened out	clear things up	talk things over
cold shoulder	left out of the picture	silent treatment

Appendix V

225 Low Cost, No Cost, Highly Effective Maverick Marketing™ Techniques

1. Ad specialties
2. Ads
3. Advertorials
4. Articles
5. Association membership
6. Audiocassettes
7. Awards
8. Balloons
9. Barter
10. Billboards (outdoor)
11. Bill paying
12. Blimps
13. Booklets
14. Books
15. Booths (kiosk)
16. Bribes (ethial)
17. Brochures
18. Bulletin boards
19. Bundling
20. Business cards
21. Business card ads
22. Business directories
23. Business meals
24. Cable TV
25. Calendar listings
26. Calendars
27. Card decks
28. Cards (birthday, thank you, holiday)
29. Catalogs
30. Celebrity endorsement
31. Centers of influence
32. Chambers of commerce
33. Charities
34. Circulars
35. Civic organizations
36. Classes (courses)
37. Classified ads
38. Clincs (how to)
39. Clothing (caps, t-shirts, jackets)
40. Club memberships
41. Column
42. Commercials
43. Committees
44. Community service
45. Competitors
46. Confirmation calls
47. Consortiums
48. Consultation
49. Contests
50. Co-op mailings
51. Co-op referral lists
52. Coupons
53. Credit cards accepted
54. Cross promotions
55. Cross selling
56. Cross training
57. Customer appreciation programs
58. Customer awards
59. Customer mailing lists
60. Customer service
61. Customer surveys
62. Demonstrations
63. Direct mail
64. Directories
65. Direct response ads
66. Discounts
67. Displays (take one)
68. Distributors
69. Donations
70. Door hangers
71. Electronic billboards
72. Electronic bulletin boards
73. Empowered employees
74. Exhibits
75. Expanded hours
76. Fairs
77. Feature stories
78. Fliers
79. FREE anything
80. Free standing inserts
81. Fundraisers
82. Gift certificates
83. Gifts
84. Give aways
85. Grand openings
86. Group mailers
87. Guarantees
88. Help lines
89. Host or hostess
90. Hours of operations
91. Image (identify)
92. Incentives
93. Independent contractors
94. In-house ad agency
95. Inserts
96. Inservice training
97. Interns
98. Invitation-only events
99. Invoice
100. Joint ventures
101. Lead boxes
102. Leads clubs
103. Lead generation
104. Letterhead
105. Letters (personalized)
106. Letter of news
107. Letters to the editor
108. Leveraging
109. Listings (directories)
110. Location
111. Logo
112. Long copy

113. Magazine ads
114. Magnetic signs
115. Mailing lists
116. Marketing plan
117. Market research
118. Marriage mailers
119. Matchbooks
120. Mentoring
121. Messages on hold
122. Mission statement(s)
123. Movie theater ads
124. Moving message displays
125. Networking
126. New business help
127. Newsletters
128. Newspaper ads
129. Niche marketing
130. Novelty items
131. Off pricing
132. One minute messages
133. On-line networking
134. Open house
135. Order forms
136. Packaging
137. Partnering
138. Party plans
139. Per inquiry advertising
140. Per order advertising
141. Personal contact
142. Personal selling
143. Piggybacking
144. Placemats
145. Point of sale display
146. Positioning
147. Postcards
148. Posters
149. Post purchase reassurance (calls and letters)
150. Premiums
151. Press (media) kit
152. Press (news) releases
153. Pricing

154. Prizes
155. Prospecting
156. Publicity
157. Public relations
158. Public Service Announcement (PSA)
159. Public speaking
160. Quality
161. Radio ads
162. Radio programs
163. Radio talk shows
164. Reactivation programs
165. Rebates
166. Recall programs
167. Recognition programs
168. Recorded messages
169. Referrals
170. Refrigerator cards
171. Refunds
172. Research reports
173. Reprints
174. Reputation
175. Restroom ads
176. Resume
177. Retention programs
178. Reward programs
179. Risk reversals
180. Sales letters
181. Sales reps
182. Sampling
183. Sandwich signs
184. Searchlight
185. Selling (direct)
186. Seminars
187. Serial appointments
188. Service recovery and restitution
189. Shopping competitors
190. Signs (indoor, outdoor, banners, window)
191. Special events
192. Special reports
193. Speeches
194. Sponsorships

195. Stamps
196. Statement stuffers
197. Stationery
198. Surveys
199. Table tents
200. Tag lines
201. Take one displays
202. Targeting
203. Telemarketing
204. Television ads
205. Testing (ads, messages, everything)
206. Testimonials
207. Tracking
208. Trade outs
209. Trade shows
210. Transit advertising
211. Unique Selling Proposition (USP)
212. Upselling (cross selling)
213. Value-added service
214. Value cards
215. Vehicle ads (magnetic signs)
216. Vendor support programs
217. Video cassette box ads
218. Videotapes
219. Volunteerism
220. Welcome wagon
221. Word of mouth
222. Workshops
2232. Yellow pages
224. 800 Telephone #
225. 900 Telephone #

And, an added bonus Maverick Marketing™ technique, one that is probably more important, more powerful and more effective than any of the other 225 listed here, YOU

ABOUT THE AUTHOR

Dr. Richard Gerson is an internationally renowned author, speaker and management consultant. He has written 11 books that have been translated into 7 foreign languages, and he has published over 200 professional and popular articles on customer service, sales, marketing, communications and management.

Richard's philosophy about presenting to an audience or consulting with a client is to always give them more than they expect. His dynamic approach involves his audience and motivates them to immediately implement his practical tips and techniques.

NOTES

NOTES

NOTES

NOTES

ABOUT CRISP PUBLICATIONS

We hope that you enjoyed this book. If so, we have good news for you. This title is only one in the library of Crisp's best-selling books. Each of our books is easy to use and is obtainable at a very reasonable price.

Books are available from your distributor. A free catalog is available upon request from Crisp Publications, Inc., 1200 Hamilton Court, Menlo Park, California 94025. Phone: (415) 323-6100; Fax: (415) 323-5800.

Books are organized by general subject area.

Computer Series

Management Training

Personal Improvement

Communications

Small Business and Financial Planning